AIC Seminar: Proceedings No. 23
ISSN 0813-7005

PREVENTING PROPERTY CRIME

Proceedings of a Seminar

held 24-25 November 1987 in Canberra

Edited by

Dennis Challinger

Australian Institute of Criminology
Canberra   A.C.T.

Published and printed by the Australian Institute
of Criminology, 10-18 Colbee Court, Phillip, A.C.T.
Australia, 2606. June 1988.

Publications resulting from seminars held by the
Australian Institute of Criminology are issued in
two series <u>AIC Seminar. Report</u> and
<u>AIC Seminar. Proceedings</u>. These replace the
former series <u>Report on Training Project</u> and
<u>Proceedings - Training Project</u>.

The National Library of Australia catalogues this
work as follows:

Preventing property crime.

   ISBN 0 642 13444 8.

   1. Crime prevention - Australia - Congresses.
   2. Offenses against property - Australia -
   Congresses. I. Challinger, Dennis.
   II. Australian Institute of Criminology.
   (Series : AIC seminar. Proceedings; no. 23).

364.4'0994

CONTENTS

OVERVIEW   1

       Dennis Challinger

OPENING ADDRESS   5

       Duncan Chappell

CRIME PREVENTION IN ENGLAND: THEMES AND ISSUES   11

       Paul Ekblom

PUBLIC TELEPHONE VANDALISM   31

       Bill Jamieson

PREVENTING CRIMINAL DAMAGE TO SCHOOLS   35

       John Allsopp

NEIGHBOURHOOD WATCH: A DISCUSSION

- ISSUES AND POLICY IMPLICATIONS   51

       Paul Wilson and Satyanshu Mukherjee

- NEIGHBOURHOOD WATCH IN AMERICA   56

       Chris Coster

- NEIGHBOURHOOD WATCH, THE ELDERLY
  AND ETHNIC COMMUNITIES   63

       Andrew Hiller

- SOCIETY'S ATTITUDE TO CRIME   64

       John Westbury

SELLING CRIME PREVENTION TO THE COMMUNITY   69

        Jim King

THE CRIME PREVENTION INDUSTRY   77

        John Hopgood

ANATOMY OF A CRIME PREVENTION PUBLICITY CAMPAIGN   85

        Laurie Monaghan

CRIME PREVENTION IN THE WORKPLACE:

•   CRIME IS A SYMPTOM, BAD MANAGEMENT THE DISEASE   95

        Ray Brown

•   A RETAIL PERSPECTIVE   101

        John Rice

PARTICIPANTS LIST   109

OVERVIEW

Dennis Challinger
Assistant Director (Information and Training)
Australian Institute of Criminology
Canberra

The major point to emerge from this Seminar was the importance of local communities in preventing property crime. For sure community vigilance and co-operation could also possibly prevent crimes against the person, but it was the more frequently occurring property crimes that were the focus for this Seminar.

Notwithstanding that, in his opening address, the Director of the Australian Institute of Criminology, Professor Duncan Chappell, provided examples of violence from around the world and compared them with the situation in Australia. He pointed out that an Australian's risk of becoming a victim of 'a burglary or property related crime' is much higher than the risk of their being the victim of a violent crime. Reducing these overall risks of victimisation would follow from the prevention of some crimes, and Professor Chappell indicated that the Institute was intending to direct more of its resources in the future towards crime prevention.

In recent years, there has been a steadily growing interest in crime prevention throughout the world. In England, it has been suggested, crime prevention has become a 'key' to the law and order question and all political parties are concerned to be seen as actively encouraging crime prevention initiatives (Morison, 1987). That political interest might be seen as explaining some of the considerable growth in the Crime Prevention Unit of the British Home Office since its inception. The work of that Unit has itself focused mostly on property crime with research reports on burglary, car theft and shop theft, and more recently robberies and juvenile crime (which is predominantly property-oriented).

Participants at the Seminar were fortunate indeed to hear Dr Paul Ekblom, now a Principal Research Officer with that Unit, discuss the various developments in crime prevention in Britain. He made particular reference to the need for information on individual offences to be gathered and subjected to careful and considered analysis before suggestions for preventive strategies were developed. That analytical stage should involve all parties to the offence so that, for example, crime on underground trains would involve not only security personnel and police but also train drivers, maintenance staff and management. That approach, Dr Ekblom pointed out, was time consuming but necessary. Only after such analysis could preventive strategies be devised, implemented and evaluated. That last stage, evaluation, was, Dr Ekblom remarked, particularly important.

Damage to public property remains an offence that continues to cause many communities harm and untold inconvenience. Two examples of this offence, vandalism to telephone boxes and schools, were discussed by Mr Bill Jamieson and Mr John Allsopp, respectively. Each indicated the considerable extent of damage to public property through vandalism and arson. Each also extolled the virtue of community co-operation in preventing further such offences. Thus, Mr Jamieson spoke of the 'adopt a phone box' campaign and Mr Allsopp spoke of evening patrols of schools by groups of parents.

Despite such initiatives, each of these speakers also emphasised that conventional security approaches were still used. Thus, Mr Jamieson spoke of staking out particularly trouble-prone phone boxes, and Mr Allsopp indicated the increased number of schools that were being provided with electronic surveillance equipment.

Neighbourhood Watch, the single most popular community crime prevention initiative in Australia, was the subject of particular discussion involving a number of Neighbourhood Watch volunteers who were present at the Seminar. Dr Paul Wilson and Dr Sat Mukherjee presented their findings of a preliminary evaluation of Victoria's Neighbourhood Watch program. Sergeant Chris Coster of the Victoria Police Neighbourhood Watch Unit commented vigorously on that evaluation before outlining his observations of Neighbourhood Watch type programs he inspected during his recent visit to Canada and the United States.

One feature of American programs to which Sergeant Coster drew particular attention was the broadening of areas of interest for Neighbourhood Watch groups. The benefit of doing that is reflected in recent research of 600 American Neighbourhood Watch programs which

> concluded that those organisations that thrived were embedded in community-linked organisations with a multi-faceted mission. This means that the healthiest 'watch' organisations embraced and advocated other issues of major community concern ranging from pot-holes to child abuse. (Calhoun, 1987, 87).

Two other police officers, Sergeant Jim King from Western Australia, and Sergeant John Hopgood from Queensland, spoke at the seminar about their considerable experience in the crime prevention field. Sergeant King described the move in his State to community policing which, he said, should involve all police being aware of, and able to offer, crime prevention advice. He indicated that the Western Australian Police Crime Prevention Bureau was now offering advice to persons who had reported burglaries to the police, and finding it most readily accepted.

Sergeant Hopgood's paper focused on the private security industry and the (crime prevention) services and devices that they provided to the community. He argued strongly for legislation to control the activities of private security operators, some of whose questionable practices he described.

The general role of the insurance industry in preventing crime was elaborated to seminar participants by Mr Colin Porter. At a practical level, Mr Laurie Monaghan traced the development of a more particular crime prevention program aimed at reducing car thefts - the Make Life Hell for Car Thieves campaign. While it was not possible for Mr Monaghan to claim that the campaign had itself caused the recent decline in car thefts in New South Wales there is little doubt that it greatly contributed to that reduction, particularly through increased public awareness following extensive media coverage.

Mr Ray Brown provided a further positive view to the seminar by discussing the particular phenomenon of theft in the workplace. He indicated how the workplace community could be used to police and prevent crime, if their working environment was such as to encourage their taking that role. Elaboration of that was given by Mr John Rice using illustrations from the retail industry. He set out a number of necessary steps that taken together would have the effect of preventing further offending.

The micro approach taken by those two speakers simply emphasised the importance of collective or community approach to crime prevention which had earlier been noted in the seminar as being the single most effective move to help prevent crime. Indeed, the benefits of this over and above an individual approach is well supported by recent research from Kentucky which found that:

> people who install alarms, leave lights and a radio on when they are away from home, lock their cars, have their valuables engraved, place warning stickers on their doors and windows and take other precautions were no less likely to be victimised than were people who did not take those measures.

While on the other hand:

> Community-wide programs such as block watches and 'establishing community areas which encourage and promote the gathering of people' have proved effective (Criminal Justice Newsletter, 1987, 6).

4

The message from that research is not that security awareness and target hardening is a waste of time, but rather that done collectively within a community, it is far more likely to achieve a reduction in crime within that community. The local experience with Neighbourhood Watch would seem to generally support that proposition. The challenge would appear to be to encourage a common attitude and approach to crime prevention across all communities in Australia.

REFERENCES

Calhoun, J.A. (1987), 'Rebuilding the Social Contract through Crime Prevention Efforts', Police Chief, September, p 87.

'Crime Prevention Measures at Household Level Found Futile', (1987), Criminal Justice Newsletter, 15 June, p 6.

Morison, J. (1987), 'New Strategies in the Politics of Law and Order', The Howard Journal, 26, pp 203-16.

Duncan Chappell
Director
Australian Institute of Criminology
Canberra

Let me welcome you to this Institute seminar on the Prevention of Property Crime and take this opportunity to say a little about the prevention of crime at large, and about the Institute's responsibilities in this area, before I introduce our keynote speaker, Dr Paul Ekblom. Of all the responsibilities that we have at the Australian Institute of Criminology none is more important than that of seeking to prevent crimes of all types. This is a responsibility that we share not just with other professionals like most of you here at this meeting, but also with all Australians because each of us has a vital interest in seeing that we live in a safe and secure environment - an environment which is to the maximum degree possible free of crime.

In the past, as we have been reminded by people like Donald Horne, we have lived in a lucky country which has remained largely immune from the crime problems that have perplexed so many other parts of the world, and particularly North America. But in recent years, as we have been informed by a veritable deluge of media reports, the state of crime in our nation has been giving cause for substantial concern. There have been troubling increases in offences against both property and violence. We have become aware of the menacing threat of drug abuse and its involvement with crime. Our naivety about organised crime and its associated corruption of our criminal justice system has been rudely shattered, and so on.

I do not wish to wallow at the outset of this seminar in the rather gloomy morass of crime statistics and crime trends with which I am sure you are all too familiar. Instead, I would like to mention some more positive and perhaps bullish developments in what has been largely a milieu pervaded by pessimism or bearish thoughts - to borrow some terminology from the stock market! Having very recently returned from a visit to North America and Europe, I am reminded of the fact that Australia still remains, in comparative terms at least, a relatively crime free, and particularly violence free society.

Let me say something first about my North American experience. I sat just ten days ago in Montreal with a group of directors of research institutes from a number of countries around the world to hear a presentation by Canadian and American criminologists on homicide, and to compare, in particular, the rates of homicide in Canada and the United States. We were provided with an extremely impressive computer-generated graphic display projected on a large screen of the actual rates of homicide in those two countries. The display showed in a dramatic way the enormous gap that exists between the rates of homicide in the United States and in its northern neighbour Canada, where I should add I have been living until very recently. The United States rate of homicide is roughly three times that of Canada. Indeed, in some American cities the actual number of homicides committed each year exceed the entire total in Canada.

Now if we had had at that presentation in Montreal figures of homicides in Australia to compare with Canada and the United States we would have seen that our rates of homicide are significantly lower than those of Canada, and certainly far below those of the United States. We would also have been able to have seen rather similar trends if we had been able to review other categories of violent crime.

Despite these observations we do tend to look towards the United States, especially, for ideas about how to prevent crime. Much of value and interest can be learned in this area from that great nation which is displaying its typical ingenuity and enthusiasm in seeking to combat many forms of criminal behaviour. But unfortunately the public enthusiasm I heard the most about in Montreal when considering the prevention of crime south of the 49th parallel related to the attraction Americans have for guns. The way in which the American nation seems to be seeking to resolve its problem with homicides and violent crime is to arm itself to a still greater degree. And the media in North America just a few days ago was replete with comments on this trend as well as a series of splashy advertisements by the National Rifle Association (NRA) which is campaigning actively to allow Americans to own more guns.

The NRA, as one commentator has suggested, is an organisation which is a master of philosophy that fits on a bumper sticker, and the bumper sticker which is now much in vogue is 'Should You Shoot a Rapist Before He Cuts Your Throat?' This slogan appeared with a large picture of a rapist with a stocking over is head in full page advertisements in liberal and conservative newspapers while I was in the United States. In small print below the NRA expanded on its theme by suggesting that Americans now lived in a society where it was pointless calling the police for help and one therefore relied on one's pistol. Equally, in interviews that were reported in some of the stories that I read, the NRA suggested that this was not a campaign to engender fear among Americans but simply to reflect the reality of what was happening. That reality can now be found in eleven American

States where citizens are allowed by law to carry concealed
handguns wherever they go. The largest of these States is
Florida which has a big urban population, and which also recently
for a short time, through a loophole which was discovered in this
law, allowed citizens to carry firearms openly. So one saw
people strolling down the streets in combat gear with their guns
swinging at their sides. Apparently because of fears that
tourism would be somewhat discouraged by this trend the Florida
legislature hastily closed the loophole. But those of you who
are thinking of visiting Disneyland in Orlando, Florida might
like to think about what people around you may still be carrying
in concealment! It's no wonder, of course, that planes are
packed with US tourists coming to Australia!

Let me switch briefly to Europe where I attended a United Nations
sponsored meeting of law enforcement experts on the subject of
the use of force and firearms by police. As soon as your
aircraft lands at Vienna you know the atmosphere is different.
You go to collect your baggage under the scrutiny of
flackjacketed paramilitary policeman who has a submachine gun
pointed at you. And round the airport are many similarly armed
officers who are there to protect you against a terrorist attack.
Of course, a very bloody terrorist attack did occur at Vienna
airport only a year ago. In fact, the meeting that I attended
with people from all over the world was surrounded by a mass of
security to protect all of us, I assume, against such threats.

I participated in a workshop which was concerned specifically
with the way in which guidelines might be developed relating to
the use of force and firearms by law enforcement officers.
Again, I could not but compare our discussions with those that
typically occur on this subject in Australia. Much of the
discussion in Vienna was about the use of firearms in crowd
control and dispersal; whether weapons should or should not be
used; whether rubber bullets, plastic bullets, or any other type
of bullet should be fired in order to get people to leave the
scene of an unlawful assembly and so on - all problems with which
we are not, fortunately, familiar. Even a democratic society
like the one that Paul Ekblom comes from is unfortunately now
having to grapple with these problems in Northern Ireland and
elsewhere.

Well, enough self-indulgence about visits to two parts of the
world. We cannot remain complacent about the levels of violence
in our society, and we have to consider how we can prevent the
still disturbing incidents of violent crime within the context of
Australia. We are not going to suggest that we arm citizens, of
course, but the Australian Institute of Criminology is involved
in a number of research and information projects which are, we
believe, contributing to the prevention of a number of forms of
violent behaviour. Let me mention very briefly several of these
projects.

The first is concerned with an examination of violence in videos. We are well aware that this is an issue of great concern to many citizens. There is a widespread belief that there is a link of some sort between consistent viewing of violence contained in videos and on television, and subsequent behaviour even though this link has not been established in a research sense. The Institute is looking at this issue and will shortly be publishing an issue of the Trends and Issues series on the subject.

We have also been involved in research on domestic violence a problem that unfortunately exists in many Australian families. In late 1985 we conducted a major national conference on this subject from which emerged a number of major recommendations about preventing violence in the family. Very recently one of our staff members has been seconded to the Office of the Status of Women within the Department of the Prime Minister and Cabinet to assist with the implementation of a national program to prevent domestic violence.

We have also been examining violence within the correctional system, and in particular have been considering the troubling questions associated with the deaths of many black Australians in custody. We will be assisting the Royal Commission that has been established on this topic.

We have also been approached by the Australian Police Association, and other community groups, about the possibility of conducting research into the use of firearms by and against police. We are giving active consideration to this suggestion.

There are other projects I could mention to you but we are, of course, here today to talk about the prevention of property crime rather than violence. Violence can obviously take place in the context of property offences. The possibility of encountering a burglar who may become a rapist or even a murderer is one that I imagine prays upon people's minds. But the risk of becoming a victim of violent crime is still very low compared with that of becoming the victim of a property offence in Australia. Less than 5 per cent of all our reported offences involve violence. The risk, on the other hand, of becoming the victim of a burglary or a related property crime is much much higher.

How can we reduce this risk? We have brought you together today to discuss this question. I should mention that in addressing this question we are at some disadvantage because we lack accurate, reliable and uniform data in Australia about crime trends and particularly trends in the area of property crime. We do not possess current data from crime surveys which could tell us about the scope and range of victimisation across the nation based on information generated not from police sources but from independent interviews conducted with individual citizens. The lack of regular crime surveys, in the view of the Institute is a serious deficiency. We are working actively at this moment to remedy the situation. Regular crime surveys would allow us to trace not only trends in crime victimisation with much greater specificity than has been possible in the past, but would also permit us to assess the effectiveness of different types of crime prevention programs, like the ones that you will be discussing here over the next two days.

In establishing what we hope will become a regular crime survey program we are very keen to encourage participation by the private sector, and insurance industry representatives especially. We welcome to this seminar members of the insurance industry who have taken a lead, in company with the police, in the crime prevention area in Australia. A number of the insurance industry's very important crime prevention initiatives will I know be discussed here over the next two days.

The police are themselves also dedicated increasingly to crime prevention and that dedication is reflected in certain police initiated programs we will be discussing. In the past I think there has been a tendency amongst police agencies to relegate crime prevention activities to a rather subsidiary status. Crime prevention units have had low status out on the streets which is 'where the action is'. Officers assigned to crime prevention units have often thought that they have been pushed to one side and are missing the opportunities that their colleagues have for doing real police work. But we are, I believe, seeing a change in that philosophy, a change that I understand is identified in Australia with an event in 1980 when the Police Commissioners of this nation adopted a logo of 'Let's Work Together'. The Commissioners agreed to place a new emphasis on community-based policing and especially on the involvement of individual citizens in the work of preventing crime. It is a trend which I think all of us should encourage and applaud. We will learn more about how this new philosophy has been working during our seminar.

Despite these encouraging trends I also understand that it has been difficult for the police of the nation who are concerned with crime prevention to act in a co-ordinated way and discuss the initiatives that they are involved with in their individual jurisdictions so as not to overlap or to find themselves competing with one another. It is for this reason pleasing that we have brought together a number of these police groups - police experts in the area of crime prevention - who will, we hope, quite apart from their presentations, be able to meet with one another, talk with one another and find out what is going on in each others agencies in crime prevention. It is through co-operation rather than competition that we can achieve crime prevention. The Institute has also brought to this seminar an expert from overseas to tell us about what is occurring in the United Kingdom on the crime prevention front. We are delighted to welcome Dr Paul Ekblom to Australia. Paul Ekblom is a Social Psychologist with a PhD from the University of London. Since 1977 he has been involved in research with the Home Office Crime Prevention Unit where I understand he is currently located. He has been involved in many innovative crime prevention initiatives which he proposes to discuss today.

CRIME PREVENTION IN ENGLAND: THEMES AND ISSUES

Paul Ekblom
Principal Research Officer
Crime Prevention Unit
Home Office
London

This paper covers what has happened in Britain over four years, a period in which crime prevention has made something of a breakthrough. It has been quite an exciting time during which an almost totally new area of government policy has appeared - a 'green field' building site for ideas. I shall deliberately avoid saying too much about specific organisations, and the bureaucratic context, because things may well be different here. Instead I shall focus on themes and issues, which are more likely to transfer to the Australian situation.

It is supposed to be obvious that 'prevention is better than cure'. It was obvious to the founding father of the Metropolitan Police, Sir Robert Peel, who wrote:

> It should be understood at the outset that the principal object to be obtained is the prevention of crime. To this great end every effort of the police is to be directed. The security of person and property...will thus be better effected than by the detection and punishment of the offender after he has succeeded in committing crime.

That was in 1829. From that high moment, crime prevention became something of a Cinderella, left behind from the Police Ball, but equally neglected by the community, who said 'it's the responsibility of the police now'. Prevention dwindled to 'lock it or lose it' publicity campaigns and casework with individual householders or companies advised about locks and bolts; there was little strategy, and solutions were taken off-the-peg rather than targeted to specific crime problems, so unsurprisingly they were rather a poor fit.

THE BREAKTHROUGH IN CRIME PREVENTION

Eight years ago I wrote a brief article called 'The crime free car', in which I discussed the scope for redesigning vehicles to make them harder to break into and illegally drive away. Absolutely nothing happened for five years. Then by 1984 everything had changed, the go-ahead was given to do some research and the end result is a series of British Standards for car security design (Southall and Ekblom, 1985). What happened?

One of the most important reasons for the breakthrough was the 'nothing works' research of the sixties and seventies, in which police patrolling, detective work, sentencing, imprisonment, and even crime prevention publicity campaigns (Burrows and Heal, 1979; Riley and Mayhew, 1980) were each in turn shown to be of relatively limited effectiveness in controlling crime. Financial constraints had in any case severely curtailed the growth in police resources that believers felt necessary to get on top of crime.

On another tack, crime surveys such as the British Crime Survey (Hough and Mayhew, 1985) have shown that a large proportion of crime never comes to the attention of the criminal justice system and so cannot be tackled by conventional means. For the final component of change, in the research world there were moves to regard criminal behaviour as something relatively normal, rather than wicked or mentally ill; and to give less emphasis to unchanging features of personality as a cause and more on social influences and pressures on offenders, together with situational opportunities for crime. By this I mean for example the presence of a vulnerable and tempting target, such as a music cassette within easy reach on a display shelf, and the absence of effective defenders. This perspective has opened up a whole new dimension of practical possibilities for prevention. Cut the opportunities and - at least in part - you cut the crime.

Together, these factors led to a reappraisal of the boundaries of responsibility for crime prevention. Rather than being the exclusive preserve of the police, it is now becoming seen as the task of whichever individuals or organisations in the community can effectively and acceptably contribute to the reduction of criminal opportunity or criminal motivation (Engstad and Evans, 1980). With the interdependency that comes with an advanced industrial society, this means a large number of people and organisations contributing in a diverse range of ways, none of which is likely to be sufficient by itself. Because of this need for co-ordination, to take the notion of shared responsibility further, a particular buzzword term has arisen - the 'multiagency approach'.

HOME OFFICE CRIME PREVENTION UNIT

In November 1983 the Home Office Crime Prevention Unit (CPU) was set up to try to pursue these themes in practical ways, building on the results of a previous program of research conducted by the Home Office Research and Planning Unit (eg Clarke and Mayhew, 1980). An early success was the Government Circular, signed by the Permanent Secretaries of the Home Office and four other government departments, addressed to the heads of a wide range of local services such as police, education and social services, recommending the new sharing of responsibility for crime prevention.

The CPU currently has five research posts (of which one is a police inspector) and about 20 clerical staff; three people are seconded from industry. Its current activity falls under seven headings:

1. to heighten public awareness of the way they can create opportunities for crime and contribute to its prevention (through a national publicity budget of some ⩵5m for TV and press campaigns and the magazine Crime Prevention News, supplemented by the contributions of local police forces and other local agencies); to demonstrate the range of activities already under way, and to encourage participation in them;

2. to foster the crime prevention element within policies of other central government departments where these have a bearing on crime (through the Ministerial Group on Crime Prevention, which involves ministers and officials from 12 departments);

3. to stimulate local crime prevention activities particularly in those areas facing social and economic difficulties (mainly involving five local demonstration projects in which the Home Office has paid for a local crime prevention co-ordinator who works with a local steering committee to identify patterns of crime and secure appropriate changes in local practice, such as in local government housing departments, leisure and shopping facilities);

4. to encourage the private sector to engage more fully in crime prevention work (for example in supporting financially, or in kind, local preventive initiatives; ensuring the goods or services they produce make crime harder to commit);

5. to advance police training in crime prevention techniques; and

6. to foster a program of research leading to new and innovative practical measures against crime.

With respect to research and development, the CPU has so far pursued the situational approach to prevention (eg Clarke, 1983) with some vigour as it enjoys a fairly strong background of basic research and can pay off in the shorter term — so I shall concentrate on this today. However, the Unit is also developing an interest in measures that rely on social/background changes to reduce criminal motivation.

The Unit publishes its research as CPU papers and these reflect the current crime prevention interest in Britain. To date the papers are entitled <u>Reducing Burglary: a study of chemists' shops</u> (Laycock, 1985), <u>Reducing Crime: developing the role of crime prevention panels</u> (Smith and Laycock, 1985), <u>Property Marking: a deterrent to domestic burglary?</u> (Laycock, 1985), <u>Designing for Car Security: towards a crime free car</u> (Southall and Ekblom, 1985), <u>The Prevention of Shop Theft: an approach through crime analysis</u> (Ekblom, 1986), <u>Prepayment Coin Meters: a target for burglary</u> (Hill, 1986), <u>Crime in Hospitals: diagnosis and prevention</u> (Smith, 1987), <u>Preventing Juvenile Crime: the Staffordshire Experience</u> (Heal and Laycock, 1987) and <u>Preventing Robberies at Sub-Post Offices: an evaluation of a security initiative</u> (Ekblom, 1987).

THE PREVENTIVE PROCESS

One of the key elements in the research and development program of the CPU is the application of what can simply be termed the 'Preventive Process'. This has originated from the <u>problem-oriented</u> approach to policing, developed by Herman Goldstein and others in North America (Goldstein, 1979). In it, the 'who' and 'how' of crime prevention (or any other policing task) are subordinated to the key question 'What is the specific and local nature of the crime problem to be dealt with?' The decision as to what preventive measures should be introduced, and by whom, is taken in the light of all available information on the problem itself and the range of solutions feasible.

The Preventive Process is a sequence of activities linked together in five stages:

- Obtaining information on crime problems
- Analysing and interpreting the information
- Devising preventive strategies
- Implementation
- Evaluation

The Preventive Process is not a set of ready-made answers to crime - it is a method for devising solutions to match problems. It is based on the assumption that crimes do not occur at random, but display distinct local patterns that reflect regularities in the real world. These can be regularities of offenders - such as concentrations of residence, motivation (such as drug addiction), habit or culture; or regularities in the environment - such as a vulnerable make of car, a poorly-protected commuter car park or hard-to-supervise hospital buildings. Identifying

these patterns and dealing with the underlying causes of crime
by a combination of situational and social/background measures
seems an almost painfully obvious thing to do, but there are
issues to face at every stage. I would like to run through some
of these in turn, so that you can be forewarned and forearmed.

ISSUES IN OBTAINING INFORMATION ON CRIME

For a number of reasons getting a sufficiently valid picture of
crime to work on, may involve some effort.

* There may be a lot of crime about - some of it quite serious,
such as sexually or racially-offensive behaviour - but not
reported to the police. Obviously, no preventive action can
sensibly be taken until some information has been obtained. This
can either be by a one-off, and expensive, crime survey; by
trying to encourage more individual victims to report; or with
corporate victims, trying to get them to routinely make
systematic records of their own. We have used this last approach
in a pair of major private shopping centres which had problems
with rowdyism, and to tackle theft in a large music shop, where
store detectives noted down details about each theft spotted.

* Where crime recording is already routine, the information noted
down will be primarily intended for administrative, detective or
prosecutional purposes - the details may not be relevant for
crime prevention, which needs for example location, circumstance
and method of offending. Information may be frustratingly terse.
Fortunately, systems in which police officers are able to enter
crime reports directly onto local terminals of the force computer
are being developed and these will allow for automatic prompting
for particular kinds of information. At the moment these are
primarily directed towards aiding detection and patrolling, but
they have obvious potential for crime prevention.

* There is also plenty of scope for bias in any recording
process, particularly where people work the rules for self-
interest. For example, some head teachers will record a case of
window breakage as 'accidental damage', to avoid besmirching
their school's name; others, presumably either very self-
confident or already fallen, may enter it as 'vandalism' in the
knowledge that this will get it repaired quicker.

ISSUES IN ANALYSING AND INTERPRETING CRIME PATTERNS

* There is often a goldmine of local crime information somewhere
in most police stations, railway operation rooms or wherever -
but like a goldmine, it may be buried under tons of
organisational rubble and may need a lot of effort to refine it.
Crime analysis is so much easier and quicker if it can be done on

information already on a computer. Only relatively simple
statistical packages are needed, and some of our police forces
have them on local microcomputers, as well as on the central
mainframe; but we are trying to develop more sophisticated
software. The first example here is a plot of burglaries by
police beat. The second one is a pinpoint plot, which shows
exactly where the offences occurred on a streetmap.

* Obviously, such facilities have to be paid for - but there is
much opportunity for sharing costs among different policing
functions. The collection and analysis of crime and incident
information can make equally important contributions to the
planning of patrol deployment, criminal investigation (for
example in analysing Modus Operandi) and targeting of offenders.

* Moving away from the hardware and software-type issues, there
are two related problems that any crime analyst has to face: the
rarity of crime, and the stability of crime patterns. Anybody
looking at aggregate crime statistics can be forgiven for
thinking that crime is happening round every corner, every day
of the week. The reality is, that on the very local level, where
many preventive schemes are pitched, crime is often so rare that
geographical patterns may be hard to establish, and hence certain
types of preventive strategies are hard to develop. This is even
the case when crime surveys supplement police figures. With
small numbers, any patterns that do emerge may be unstable from
year to year - again a poor basis for devising preventive
strategies, and an absolute bugbear of evaluation.

ISSUES IN GENERATING PREVENTIVE IDEAS

* The analysis complete, the main task in generating preventive
ideas is to break out of fixed thinking. You can help the
creative process by working down a list of basic types of
preventive measure and seeing which can be made to apply in the
present circumstances - such as 'removal of target',
'surveillance by employees', and so forth. Another tack is to
put yourself in the position of the offender, and to identify the
logistical steps necessary to carry through a crime, in order to
find out which points to block. With robbers on the London
Underground, for example, the logistical stages are something
like this:

Stages of a Robbery on the Tube

    1. Entry into underground system
    2. Travel to hunting ground
    3. Waiting or circulation at hunting ground
    4. Sussing out victim and circumstances
    5. Closing in/preparation

6. Striking at victim
7. Pressing home attack
8. Flight
9. Return to 3 or exit system.

It is often useful in exploring such logistical issues to speak
to a sample of offenders about what opportunities they see, what
decisions they take, what risks they face and how they cope with
them. Some contract researchers are doing it for me at the
moment, with robbers, pickpockets and assailants on the
Underground. Bennett (1986) has done a similar thing with
burglars, for example showing them videos of residential streets
and getting them to talk through their decisions.

* Whatever the source of one's ideas, they must be put together
in a way that avoids vulnerabilities that the criminal will
continue to exploit. For example, there is little to be gained
by strengthening the front doors on houses if the frames are left
weak; and it is similarly pointless to fit windowlocks if the
householders don't bother to shut the windows when they go out.
The whole target has to be treated like a complete system,
including the human components as well as the physical ones, and
an equally comprehensive package must be put together for
prevention (Southall and Ekblom, 1985; Pease, 1987).

* It is vital that people from all levels participate in the
planning process, perhaps in some kind of working group. This
not only means that the experience and the insights of staff at
the workface are tapped – after all, these are the people who
actually know what it's like to face an aggressive passenger, or
repair a vandalised phone box – but it also means that they will
have some sense of 'ownership' for the project, and their
commitment may be the key to successful implementation.

* Anybody can generate a whole string of preventive ideas, but
not all of them will be of much practical use. Experience shows
that even the most simple and attractive ideas can fall on a
number of grounds such as cost of equipment or personnel;
interference with the main activity of the organisation, such as
selling goods or running trains on time; and safety. Now is the
time to work down the initial list of ideas, filtering out those
that cannot pass this elementary test of practicality, and
adapting others to fit. At this point, the working group should
have a set of fairly well developed ideas ready to sell to senior
management – and 'sell' it is, because a well-considered and
costed case is the only way to overcome disinterest in crime
prevention and get the go-ahead. In the case of shop theft, I
had to educate myself not only in the world of the store
detective, but also in the world of retail management, to be able
to talk persuasively to them in their own terms, ranging from

masterbags, gondolas and browsers to 'return on investment', and find ways of making crime prevention mesh with the rest of their policies.

ISSUES IN IMPLEMENTATION

The implementation stage is often the most protracted, and the most demanding of persistence, co-ordination and troubleshooting (Hope, 1985). For example in trying to get a number of security schemes going on the London Underground (see Department of Transport, 1986), such as the provision of passenger alarms on platforms and enhanced CCTV, people from Operations, Signalling, Engineering, Permanent Way, Marketing and Personnel all needed to be repeatedly consulted as the plans progressed. There are natural channels in such organisations for, say, the prevention of physical accidents; but the prevention of crime was a complete new function which had to be threaded through the maze of competing considerations. It has been a bit like rewiring an old house.

* Many attempts to inject crime prevention into large organisations have failed because, in organisational terms, they have rather naively been 'bolted on' to an otherwise unchanged structure, for example as a special project, and just as readily drop off when the project is over. This occurred with the NACRO safe neighbourhood projects which aimed to improve the quality of life on 'problem housing estates' in Britain (Osborn, 1987). Considerable gains are apparently made during the lifetime of the project, but soon after the external co-ordinator and the special funds are withdrawn, things quickly lose momentum. What may be needed to permanently foster crime prevention in, say, local government, is an official permanently responsible for keeping it alive, with adequate facilities and a committee of elected council members to tackle key policy decisions and provide support against the inevitable barrage of competing demands for resources from roads, sewerage, libraries, environmental health and so on.

* Salesmanship obviously continues during implementation, and acceptable ways have to be found of overcoming resistance to crime prevention. Car manufacturers have not been keen to take on board the extra constraints of making their vehicles 'crime-free', and have pointed to the lack of consumer demand for security, and to even slight increases in production cost reducing their competitiveness against their rivals in a saturated market. We found the best approach to these obstacles was to turn them to our advantage — by awakening public expectations that manufacturers can, and ought, to do something about security, and to set the companies competing against one another on the security reputations of their products. This is beginning to bear fruit in that we are seeing a growing trickle

of car advertisements in which security is featured; and the consumer magazine 'Which?' has published a survey of vulnerable models.

ISSUES IN EVALUATION

Assume a hypothetical preventive scheme has been running for some months, teething troubles have been solved and crime appears to be falling in the right places. But has it really worked? Is it worthwhile continuing? And can it be adopted elsewhere? Deceptively simple questions like these have provoked the fiercest arguments among researchers, and the strongest clashes between researchers and practitioners. Evaluation is important in crime prevention, not only to aid the individual local decision-maker in using limited resources to best effect, but as a means of contributing to a collective body of reliable knowledge on what works under what circumstances, and what is a waste of time. We are still at the beginning of this process, although there are plenty of 'pop' crime prevention ideas going the rounds as the demand exceeds supply.

The first question in any evaluation is simply 'has there been a real change in crime levels, rather than random fluctuation?' - and here, the small numbers of crimes at the local level mean that with preventive schemes centring around particular troublespots, it is very hard to give a certain answer. Paradoxically, I suspect that the smaller-scale schemes (such as miniature neighbourhood watch groups) are likely to have a more powerful effect than larger schemes (such as district-wide neighbourhood watch), but changes in crime levels are easier to detect in the larger ones.

The second question is, given a 'real' drop in crime levels, how far can this be accredited to the security initiative, as opposed to the hundred and one alternative causal explanations such as a lucky break by the police, or bad weather? Evaluations are usually such a mess of complications that the answer is never remotely 100 per cent certain (see Ekblom, 1987).

The clashes I referred to can be spectacular. I have seen professional researchers all but lynched by enthusiastic crime prevention activists who have just been told that their cherished publicity campaigns, or neighbourhood watch scheme, has had no effect on crime. The researchers may be correct, for practitioners can sometimes be accused of viewing their schemes through rosy-tinted spectacles and succumbing to elementary methodological pitfalls such as tiny numbers or regression to the status quo. However, in my experience many researchers err too far on the 'nothing works' side, carrying over 'academic' standards of statistical significance testing to a context of practical decision-making where practitioners cannot take the

researcher's 'don't know' for an answer and are prepared to
tolerate a greater risk of the conclusion being wrong; for them,
the worst state is indecision. Airing these issues of
uncertainty and standards of inference early in a project is the
only satisfactory way for a researcher to work with
practitioners.

THE EFFECTIVENESS OF CRIME PREVENTION

The central question of whether prevention works raises the vexed
question of displacement - are we merely shifting crime from one
patch to another, or from one method to another? My shop theft
research involved the HMV Shop, a large four-floored department
store on London's premier shopping street, Oxford Street (Ekblom,
1986). Here, the security initiative involved installing a
sticky-label alarm system, resiting the browser shelves to aid
surveillance and closing down the heavily-hit computer tapes
section of the store. The rate of arrest of shop thieves has
decreased by half since it started. Most of the drop in arrests
can be attributed to the security initiative, and it is possible
to argue that the drop also reflects changes in the true crime
rate. There is some evidence of partial displacement to other
music stores on Oxford Street - but does it matter? From the
individual store's point of view, this is ideal - drive the
thieves away to plague the competitors! But from the perspective
of the public interest, if all the exercise does is to shift some
of the crime around a little, the effort may have been rather
wasted. But we cannot tell until all the music shops tighten
their security to the same degree - at the moment we have one
hard target and a lot of softer ones. It is probable that
reducing the overall level of theft on Oxford Street will involve
three steps forward and one step back - tightening up store
number one moves some, but not all, of the crime to the most
vulnerable of the rest of the stores; tightening these in their
turn reduces overall crime further but moves some onto the third
band, and so on. At each stage, one hopes, some of the thieves
drop out of the game altogether as risk and effort grow too large
in relation to reward.

But in some circumstances moving the crime around may even be a
desirable goal in itself. Lightning may not strike the same
place twice, but house burglary apparently does - and often the
households involved may be disadvantaged in other ways, such as
suffering unemployment or being single-parent families. It may
be socially just to target preventive resources such as lock,
door and window improvements on these already-burgled people,
just to spread the misery round (Pease, 1987). And government
may also see fit to intervene to restore a level of equity if we
have a situation where the well-off can afford to buy security
and hence displace burglary onto the poor.

Another example of a successful preventive scheme is an attempt
by our Post Office to control a wave of robberies at the smaller
branches in London. Analysis of the Post Office's own crime
records showed that many of the robberies involved sledgehammer
attacks on the anti-bandit screens and exploitation of insecure
doors and hatches, so the Post Office embarked on a program of
upgrading the screens in all 1300 branches, with security
training for the staff.

I evaluated this initiative (Ekblom, 1987), and to cut a very
long story short, the good news was that altogether an estimated
75 incidents a year were prevented, of which 45 would have
involved substantial loss. As might be expected, the preventive
effect showed up most in the physical attacks and those
exploiting insecurity. The bad news however was that the robbers
resorted to other methods, in most cases a simple firearms threat
at the screen; but the silver lining to this cloud was that
altogether twice as many of these 'displaced' incidents were
failures as successes, with the robbers being scared off empty-
handed. I should mention that most of the physical and
insecurity attacks had involved guns anyway, but only in a
supporting role, rather than centre stage. Many critics of
situational crime prevention claim that it cannot tackle serious
crime such as robbery, where offenders are seen as professional
and highly motivated to succeed. But in this case many of the
offenders seemed inept and amateurish people who believed
possession of a gun and physical fitness could substitute for
planning and courage, and many of their attempts ended in farce.

Success stories such as these should not blind us to the
probability that any one preventive measure may have only a
limited useful life. Post Office robbers may eventually find new
ways of attacking their targets and another initiative will be
needed. There will be an inevitable lag between the emergence
of a new pattern and the Post Office's ability to detect the
change reliably enough to act, to decide what to do and to
implement this. Routine monitoring of the crime problem, aided
by computerised incident logging and analysis, can keep this lag
to a minimum.

Perhaps the best example of limited life comes in the area of the
crime-free car (Southall and Ekblom, 1985). The impact of
steering column locks on car theft had begun to wear off in the
early 1980s, just a few years after their introduction. Apart
from the effects of wear in making the locks easier to jiggle,
thieves had developed techniques for overcoming them, and the
existence of a regulation specifying the lock in some detail had
absolved manufacturers from trying to improve upon it - rather,
they tended to 'design down' to the standard. Crime prevention
here can be seen as a kind of 'arms race', in which thieves and
designers are constantly struggling to get a momentary advantage.

22

As an example of the ingenuity of car thieves in this respect, I heard of a German car whose central locking system worked on compressed air lines. Thieves discovered that if you cut a hole in a tennis ball, fitted it over the outside keyhole and gave it a thump, the locks all obligingly flew open. To keep up with the thieves, the police need to collate information such as this and feed it to the car designers as fast as new patterns can be discovered.

CONFLICTING CONSTRAINTS

I'd like to look at a few broader issues. Crime prevention is a newcomer in an area where territory was long ago carved up between, for example, fire regulations, road and rail safety, public health and planning controls. As such it is at a severe disadvantage when regulations conflict, because unlike these others it never has any statutory force behind it. Fire regulations, for example, are quite powerful in Britain and are designed to make it easy for people to leave burning buildings in a hurry. They naturally tend to clash with crime prevention requirements which try to make it harder for people to get in — or out with their spoils. Prevention may also conflict with less formally-supported principles such as aesthetics (hideous grilles and bolts; public parks without bushes and winding paths), convenience (some window locks can be a pain and cease to be used), privacy (neighbourhood watch means surrendering some), reliability (there's nothing more infuriating than a dud entryphone or an over-sensitive car alarm) and peace of mind (with some people overt security measures can keep fear of crime alive). Business people legitimately worry that preventive action can lose them sales — by taking up space, putting off legitimate customers, occupying staff time. And to many people, preventive measures will have a significant financial cost. Finally, prevention can conflict with broader policy considerations such as subsidies for public transport to provide a get-you-home service after pubs and club close — if they don't run, cars will probably be stolen.

Obviously, we can't have our cake and eat it, and a sensible balance must be struck between the priorities of crime prevention and these other important considerations. But we can have more of our cake, and eat more of it, by alerting the right people in the right places to the need to consider crime prevention, and by careful design. The essence of good design, whether of car locks or housing policies, sales methods or bus schedules, is the reconciliation of conflicting constraints. The crime free car research showed that it was possible to thread crime prevention between the half-dozen conflicting and competing principles that underlie vehicle design, at a price that car buyers would countenance. As a consequence, the British Standards Institute is now introducing a series of design standards on car security (similar standards have been introduced for housing design).

Where crime prevention does not actually conflict with other considerations, but merely competes for resources, a good way of reducing cost is piggybacking on facilities used mainly for other purposes. In a big store, slotting the preventive function into a computerised point of sale bar code system of stock control is one example that involves little cost but enables management to pinpoint the sources of loss; it parasitises existing arrangements.

CONFLICTING INTEREST GROUPS

'The Community', with which we aim to share responsibility for crime prevention, is far from the image many people have of something warm, embracing and homogeneous – a kind of social porridge. As anybody who tries to get involved with it will know, there are differences of interest at every level of the community, into which crime prevention treads at its peril – below the surface, the porridge is seething and probably shark-infested!

Crime prevention can sometimes add to conflict – one person's car alarm is the neighbour's disturbed night. Sometimes prevention can resolve conflict, by finding kids somewhere off the street to play where they won't disturb elderly residents. As another example, the HMV shop theft project I worked on highlighted a conflict between the taxpayer and a store, which wanted to maximise sales and minimise costs by putting cassettes in their containers on the shelves, in so-called 'live displays', rather than keep them behind the counter. The cassettes, of course, tempted thieves as much as they tempted legitimate purchasers, and the store chose to try to control the crime by employing large numbers of store detectives and referring nearly every arrest to the police. At one stage the HMV Shop accounted for 40 per cent of the entire shoplifter intake to the police from the whole of Oxford Street, which is over a mile long and jammed with department stores.

As a taxpayer itself, a store obviously has the right to expect support from the police – but only up to a limit. There comes a point when it has made crime so easy, in the name of boosting sales, that it can be regarded as negligent. When I made a comment along these lines, in the published report, I touched a raw nerve – I got a blistering review in The Grocer magazine, and a supermarket manager from Cornwall wrote to his MP to demand that I be sacked – quickly! I'm still at my job, though, and about 4,000 copies of the report have been distributed, mostly on demand. There's no such thing as bad publicity.

To reduce the crime, it would have been easy to advise the store to abandon the live display system and put the cassettes behind the counter - but this would have hit sales harder than losses and would not remotely have appealed to 'enlightened self-interest'. What I did instead was to try to devise ways of controlling theft which on the one hand allowed the store to keep the live display which was so good for profit, and on the other, avoided generating the anti-social by-product of large numbers of arrests, mostly of young people, and costing £100 a time in police resources to deal with. I have described the measures already, and the evidence that crime has been substantially reduced. But it is worth adding here that rather than feeling constrained by the new security measures, the store actually feels <u>liberated</u> by it - the alarm system has enabled them to put dearer video cassettes on live display.

CONFLICTING ORGANISATIONAL RESPONSIBILITIES AND PERSPECTIVES

The multiagency approach to prevention brings with it a number of tricky issues in the form of conflicting organisational responsibilities and perspectives. One major divide, of course, is between the law-enforcement approach of the police, and the offender-centred approach of probation officers and social workers. Housing, recreation and planning departments will also have their distinct priorities, and ways of working; add to this organisational boundaries that do not match, and the sheer task of co-ordination can be awesome. Any multiagency project, such as one aimed at reducing burglary by drug abusers, involves the exchange of information. But what information can acceptably be passed from say a drugs clinic to the police or probation service, or vice versa? Probably not information that can be pinned down to identifiable individuals. There are a lot of confidences to protect, and it is insufficient for people in friendly working relationships simply to fudge things and say 'have a cup of tea and take a look through these files, off the record'. Obviously information does need to be pooled to generate sensible strategies, but a clear code of practice needs to be developed about what it is proper to show to whom. In one multiagency project apparently the only person who commanded trust from all parties, including offenders, was a local psychiatrist, and it became his task to cross-link information on crime with information on drug addicts, remove identifying details and hand the overall pattern of results to the other agencies for action.

In the first flush of enthusiasm for a multiagency project it is very easy to be blind to the difficulties. But it is far better to have them up-front.

ACCOUNTABILITY

Issues such as the exchange of confidential information, joint budgeting and joint action, the involvement of representatives of the residents or commerce and the setting of priorities mean that some avenue of accountability is needed, whether through existing forums or through specially set up steering groups. Accountability is commonly thought of as constraining, and it does have this purpose - but it can also be liberating, giving a working group a writ to explore activities they could not otherwise have contemplated; and promoting acceptance of preventive schemes that may otherwise be seen as interfering with people's liberty, privacy or special interests.

In summary. Crime prevention is no longer the inoffensive and neutral activity it once was in the days when it consisted purely of publicity exhorting people to lock it or lose it, and advice from the police on bolts and bars. Now, it involves the police and central/local government seeking to influence the civil behaviour of particular individuals, private companies and local authority departments responsible for the creation of criminal opportunities or motivation; instead of tackling 'the common enemy, crime', it cuts across conflicting public and private interests and policies, and has to compete for resources with other goals and needs, not always as a front runner. Reconciliation of all this conflict and competition means that crime prevention has to be slipped in by changing attitudes and expectations, good salesmanship, clever design, close attention to cost effectiveness, sometimes piggybacking on other facilities and changes in an organisation, and using data recording systems developed and maintained primarily for other purposes. I have rather deliberately tended to stress the difficulties, and I am presenting a view of a hard and challenging future - but I believe it shows crime prevention has got its teeth firmly locked into the real world; that crime prevention is coming of age.

REFERENCES

Bennett, T. (1986), 'Situational crime prevention from the offenders' perspective', in K. Heal and G. Laycock (eds), Situational Crime Prevention: from Theory into Practice, HMSO, London.

Burrows, J. and Heal, K. (1979), 'Police car security campaigns', in J. Burrows, P. Ekblom and K. Heal, Crime Prevention and the Police, Home Office Research Study 55, HMSO, London.

Clarke, R. (1983), 'Situational crime prevention: its theoretical basis and practical scope', in M. Tonry and N. Morris (eds), Crime and Justice: An Annual Review of Research, 4, 225-256, University of Chicago Press, Chicago.

Clarke, R. and Mayhew, P. (eds) (1980), Designing out Crime, HMSO, London.

Department of Transport (1986), Crime on the London Underground, HMSO, London.

Ekblom, P. (1986), The Prevention of Shop Theft: An Approach Through Crime Analysis, Crime Prevention Unit Paper 5, Home Office, London.

Ekblom, P. (1987), Preventing Robberies at Sub-Post Offices: An Evaluation of a Security Initiative, Crime Prevention Unit Paper 9, Home Office, London.

Engstad, P. and Evans, J. (1980), 'Responsibility, competence and police effectiveness in crime control', in R. Clarke and J.M. Hough (eds), The Effectiveness of Policing, Gower, Farnborough.

Goldstein, H. (1979), 'Improving policing: a problem-oriented approach', Crime and Delinquency, 25, 236-258.

Heal, K. and Laycock, G. (1987), Preventing Juvenile Crime: The Staffordshire Experience, Crime Prevention Unit Paper 8, Home Office, London.

Hill, N. (1986), Prepayment Coin Meters: A Target for Burglary, Crime Prevention Unit Paper 6, Home Office, London.

Hope, T. (1985), Implementing Crime Prevention Measures, Home Office Research Study 86, HMSO, London.

Hough, J.M. and Mayhew, P. (1985), Taking Account of Crime: Key Findings From the Second British Crime Survey, HMSO, London.

Laycock, G. (1985), Reducing Burglary: A Study of Chemists' Shops, Crime Prevention Unit Paper 1, Home Office, London.

Laycock, G. (1985), Property Marking: A Deterrent to Domestic Burglary?, Crime Prevention Unit Paper 3, Home Office, London.

Osborn, S. (1987), 'Implementing change', Paper presented at British Criminology Conference, Sheffield, July 1987, (contact author at NACRO, 169 Clapham Rd, London, SW9 OPU).

Pease, K. (1987), 'Research on burglary', paper presented at British Criminology Conference, Sheffield, July 1987, (contact author at Dept of Social Administration, Manchester University, Manchester M13 9PL).

Riley, D. and Mayhew, P. (1980), Crime Prevention Publicity: An Assessment, Home Office Research Study 63, HMSO, London.

Smith, L.J.F. (1987), Crime in Hospitals: Diagnosis and Prevention, Crime Prevention Unit Paper 7, Home Office, London.

Smith, L.J.F. and Laycock, G. (1985), Reducing Crime: Developing the Role of Crime Prevention Panels, Crime Prevention Unit Paper 2, Home Office, London.

Southall, D. and Ekblom, P. (1985), Designing for Vehicle Security: Towards a Crime Free Car, Crime Prevention Unit Paper 4, Home Office, London.

*   *   *   *   *   *

DISCUSSION

Q: How do you stimulate crime prevention at the local level?

Ekblom: In England the Home Office appoints a co-ordinator, who is responsible for establishing a local crime prevention committee from members of the community. That committee includes local police, and the first thing it does is analyse the local crime data and establish where the problems are. The committee then undertakes an activist role with a broad general remit. It may, for instance, pressure electricity and gas suppliers to remove coin meters (a popular target for thieves). It may arrange for the maintenance of locks on housing estates or encourage the establishment of Neighbourhood Watch schemes. In fact, it develops a range of local crime prevention initatives.

Q: Those committees would need close liaison with local police. Do they suggest to the police that they need more police on the beat rather than mobile patrols?

Ekblom: They could express opinions which the police might consider. But remember, the evidence is that general police patrols do not have a major impact on local crime levels, although they do lessen local fear of crime.

Q: The research that is based on the views of convicted offenders does not seem very reliable. Why would those offenders bother telling the truth?

Ekblom: There are problems with that sort of research. However, we're trying to tap offenders' expertise and talk to them about their methods. Why they got involved in crime or their ideas about it are not particularly useful. It is true convicted offenders are not completely representative of all offenders, but they do have certain skills and are often keen to 'show off'.

The results of such research are often quite amazing. For instance, offenders who rob people on the street - muggers - say they like to have a moderate number of people around as they believe the victim is less likely to fight back, thinking that bystanders will help. They usually do not!

Q: One of the crime prevention videos you screened shows burglars in striped jumpers and masks. That sort of mentality distracts from other consumer rip-offs, like frauds and false insurance claims. It also encourages fear of crime and self-protection.

Ekblom: Yes, that particular video does stereotype the burglar, but it is plainly a light-hearted approach to encouraging people to safeguard their own property. On the video issues, I concede that we have to change people's views about what constitutes crime. That takes us into the political arena.

Having said that, we have done research leading to the revision of customs forms relating to importing foreign cars into Britain. Tightening up the paper work has, in fact, stopped massive losses of taxes by the Government.

Q: Where do you get the statistics you use to analyse particular crime problems?

Ekblom: While the Home Office collects national criminal statistics, it is often difficult to get local statistics without their being specially extracted.

Q: Is there a need for additional statistics?

Ekblom: Yes, in some ways. For instance, while police can give general statistics on car theft they do not have details of the model and year of car in their computer. Industry groups, however, do have records of all models on the road and one could, in theory, generate 'stealability' rates for all cars on the roads.

Q: The work you are engaged in has political overtones.
         Doesn't that make your work difficult?

Ekblom: To some extent that is true, but because crime affects
         everybody, crime prevention is seen as important.
         Nevertheless, in some left-wing controlled councils
         there is such a concern that local government should run
         crime prevention that there has at been at least one
         instance where a council has refused to allow
         Neighbourhood Watch signs to be put up.

         We have tried to overcome some local differences by
         spreading crime prevention activities around the
         country. The five-towns project is the best example of
         that.

Q: How did the Government react to the negative results of
         your research into crime prevention posters?

Ekblom: That part of the Home Office that runs publicity
         campaigns was not pleased by our negative findings.
         Such campaigns are, of course, a visible demonstration
         that the Government is active against crime. However,
         in our part of the Home Office, we're moving to the
         general idea that people themselves can do something
         about crime.

NOTE: Dr Ekblom also answered a number of questions on
         Neighbourhood Watch in England. These are included in
         the later section on that topic at page 67.

PUBLIC TELEPHONE VANDALISM

Bill Jamieson
Chief Security Officer
Telecom Australia
Melbourne

Taking the definition of vandalism as the wanton or malicious destruction or damage of property, public telephone vandalism continues to be a serious concern for Telecom and the community. Vandal damage costs are currently running at about $18.25 million per year and increasing. This damage not only adds to the telephone bill of every Telecom customer, but frequently severs a vital emergency communication link.

THE EXTENT OF THE PROBLEM

Telecom currently spends about $50 million annually to provide 32,000 public telephones for the community. Vandalism to those telephones averages $1,500 for each with the total component costs as follows:

Damage to equipment and cabinet	$6.50m
Purchase of special equipment	$ 2.50m
Cost of labour for repairs	$ 4.63m
Loss of Call Revenue	$ 2.12m
Operator service costs	$ 2.40m
Theft of money	$ 0.10m
Total	$18.25m

The more common types of damage sustained are:

- Glass breakage and cabinet damage.
- Handset damage.
- Damage to the dial or casing.
- Theft of or damage to the coin-tin.
- Theft, burning or damaging telephone books.

However, there have been a number of unusual attacks. At one time it seemed to be popular to destroy public telephone boxes with oxy-acetylene equipment. One would think that would have been fairly obvious behaviour but few such incidents were reported in time to detain offenders. Explosives have also been used to completely destroy public telephone boxes...for no apparent reason.

Why public telephones are targets for vandalism is a somewhat vexed question. Certainly they are:

- Readily available;
- Public property and therefore 'fair game';
- Often damaged in the course of an attack on the coin-tin.

Added to which is the fact that, in the past, there has been a fairly small chance of the offender being apprehended. That makes it difficult to talk with confidence about the characteristics of telephone vandals. At present around 500 offenders are detected and proceeded against each year. Telecom's experience is that those offenders tend to be bored, thrill-seeking and possibly angry youths.

RESPONDING TO VANDALISM

Telecom continues work to combat public telephone vandalism. Three main approaches – awareness campaigns, improved detection of offenders and preventive measures are currently in use.

Awareness Campaigns are firstly directed at the general public at large. Emphasising through the media the importance of the public telephone as a 'lifeline' for emergencies or for those in personal distress, is an important part of those campaigns. If that fact is appreciated by the community, there should be less calculated damage. Some Neighbourhood Watch groups have recently been enlisted to take an active part in fighting public telephone vandalism. In addition stickers are now being placed on damaged public telephones after damage to them is assessed, indicating that action is under way to repair that damage. This indicates to the public not only the fact that vandalism has occurred but also that Telecom is trying to repair the damage as fast as possible.

Separate awareness programs are undertaken for school students and police. In schools the 'lifeline' aspect is again emphasised. Interestingly, most students are quite angry about telephone vandalism and their suggestions for dealing with offenders reflect this rejection of the activity. With respect to police, Telecom security staff work closely to identify particularly popular networks of attack to alert police to current problems, and encourage them to recognise patterns of offending.

Improved detection of offenders follows from increased public reporting of offences in progress or descriptions of offenders after the event. This is happening partly as a result of the public awareness activities and partly as a result of the use of rewards. Up to $2,000 can now be paid to any member of the public assisting Telecom and it is not now necessary for an offender to be convicted in court before a reward is paid.

Within Telecom special investigative groups have been established to target particularly vandal-prone public telephones. These have been surprisingly successful and while 'staking out' trouble spots may seem a somewhat extravagant use of manpower the results justify the approach.

Many of the preventive measures are particularly apparent to users of public telephone boxes. The replacement of glass with wire-mesh in the lower walls of some phone boxes, the use of polycarbonate windows and changing designs of green telephone units are among them. However not at all visible are electronic sensors which send signals to the nearest police station when tampering occurs.

The introduction of a new coin-box design invented by a Telecom engineer Alan Kirk has been particularly successful. So far the Kirk safe has proved itself resistant to attack by oxy acetylene equipment, hydraulic jacks, Ramset guns and bricks. However a different way to make public telephones unattractive to destructive thieves (if not vandals) is the introduction of 'card phones'. These phones are operated with a plastic credit card and have been introduced as a trial in Victoria and Western Australia. It is not intended that they should completely replace coin operated public telephones as the 'lifeline' function of phones is more likely to be required when coins rather than cards are available.

In some cases, prevention of vandalism can only be achieved by re-siting particularly vulnerable public telephones. Thus some telephone boxes have been moved to more brightly lit streets or major roads where offenders would be more visible. Other phone boxes which have been found to be uneconomic have simply been removed altogether.

All these described activities are aimed at reducing the amount of public telephone vandalism around Australia. Achieving that would reduce a substantial burden on the Australian taxpayer. In turn, taxpayers can assist Telecom (and themselves) by keeping an eye on public telephone boxes and reporting any suspicious activities in, or near, them.

* * * * * *

DISCUSSION

Q: Just how does the reward scheme work?

Jamieson: Basically three levels of rewards are given. The
          first is where a member of the public provides any
          information that leads to the identification of a public
          telephone vandal. At the moment, a reward of up to $500
          would be offered under those circumstances.

          An increased reward might follow if the citizen went to a
          little more trouble and, say, followed the offender or
          gave evidence in court. At the top level are citizens
          who may have put themselves at some risk or actually
          sustained injury.

Q: There has been recent publicity to the effect that
          rewards are not being paid.

Jamieson: All bureaucracies sometimes have problems.

Q: But rewards alone are not going to stop vandalism are
          they?

Jamieson: No. And that is why we have a range of approaches,
          including the adopt-a-phone box program.

Ekblom: In England we have schemes where local councils will
          allot money to schools for their extra curricular use.
          The costs of repairing any vandalism in the local area
          are then subtracted from that pool of money. Have you
          considered such a scheme?

Jamieson: We do not have local government with those sorts of
          powers, so could not do it in Australia.

Q: Would the privatisation of public phones have any impact
          on the problem?

Jamieson: I doubt it. Each public telephone at the moment is
          costing $1,500 - $1,600 a year in repair costs. There is
          no question of public telephones making money, so they
          would probably be unattractive to private entrepreneurs.

PREVENTING CRIMINAL DAMAGE TO SCHOOLS

John Allsopp
Director, Properties
Department of Education
New South Wales

BACKGROUND

The estimated cost of repairing or replacing burnt and vandalised
school buildings and their contents in New South Wales is
$16 million per annum. This is broken down into two categories,
vandalism and theft accounting for approximately $9 million, and
arson, including the cost of repairing or replacing buildings and
their contents, the remaining $7 million. These figures are
calculated as an annual average, varying in some instances as the
result of a major fire, such as the recent destruction of Narooma
High School on the South Coast at an estimated cost of
$6 million.

Table 1 shows statistics for fires in schools month by month from
July 1985 to September 1987, indicating only the cost of damage
to buildings, contents not being included in these figures.

TABLE 1

COSTS OF FIRES IN NSW SCHOOLS (BUILDINGS ONLY)

MONTH	NO.	1985/86 ESTIMATED COST $	NO.	1986/87 ESTIMATED COST $	NO.	1987/88 ESTIMATED COST $
JULY	18	426,350	10	184,300	8	814,539
AUGUST	17	199,250	9	279,500	16	6,709,800
SEPTEMBER	10	90,900	9	149,000	8	210,500
OCTOBER	11	254,500	17	332,780		
NOVEMBER	12	181,350	14	2,271,300		
DECEMBER	6	524,000	7	72,300		
JANUARY	8	127,700	10	108,500		
FEBRUARY	13	96,400	4	200,000		
MARCH	17	384,300	5	41,000		
APRIL	14	119,950	3	33,000		
MAY	15	725,000	8	130,000		
JUNE	17	956,000	15	1,170,000		
TOTAL	158	4,085,700	111	4,971,680	32	7,734,839

The replacement of facilities destroyed by fire involves the normal processes of planning and construction, and thus, the time between the loss of a major facility, such as an Industrial Arts complex or an Administration block, and its permanent replacement, is often many weeks.

While these crimes against school property are obviously serious in terms of the economic cost to the community as a whole, they go far beyond this in terms of their cost to those directly involved in the school (students, staff, parents and friends of the school community), to whom the loss of personal property and facilities is often not nearly as devastating as the loss of morale and the feeling of futility which often follows such events.

TABLE 2

BREACHES OF SECURITY IN NSW SCHOOLS, SEPTEMBER 1987

CATEGORY	NO. OF INCIDENTS
Simple Illegal Entry	50
Vandalism	17
Theft	5
Arson	4
Attempted Arson and Vandalism	2
Illegal Entry and Vandalism	57
Illegal Entry and Theft	94
Illegal Entry and Arson	1
Illegal Entry, Vandalism and Theft	82
Illegal Entry, Vandalism and Arson	1
Illegal Entry, Vandalism, Theft and Arson	2
Illegal Entry, Theft and Arson	0
Vandalism and Theft	0
Vandalism, Theft and Arson	0
Theft and Arson	0
TOTAL	**315**

Table 2 gives details of reported breaches of security for the State in September 1987, showing the category of the offence and giving the number of incidents of each category. Such tables are recorded for each month and, together, form a profile of property crime in schools over a twelve month period. The growth of such crime is apparent from Table 3 which details the number of breaches of security submitted by NSW School Principals from 1971/72 to 1986/87.

TABLE 3

BREACHES OF SECURITY IN NSW SCHOOLS 1971-1987

YEAR	NO. OF REPORTS RECEIVED
1971/72	1542
1972/73	1852
1973/74	1947
1974/75	1900
1975/76	2176
1976/77	2243
1977/78	2641
1978/79	2560
1979/80	3021
1980/81	3092
1981/82	3448
1982/83	3575
1983/84	3794
1984/85	3872
1985/86	4366
1986/87	4515

The NSW Department of Education is divided into ten Regions, divided between Metropolitan Sydney and country areas. The security problem is most serious in Metropolitan Sydney, particularly in the west and south west, and, to a lesser extent, the east. Population density and rapid growth areas afford a major contributing factors.

COMBATING SCHOOL PROPERTY CRIME

The Department of Education has adopted a range of strategies to combat the serious social problem of property crime against schools. In recognition of the need for improved physical security in schools, the State Government has undertaken to spend $10 million per annum over a four year period to provide electronic surveillance, installation of non-urban local alarms, increased security patrols, improved physical security measures and support staffing.

When making the joint announcement with the Treasurer, the Minister for Education stated that the Department of Education had concentrated its security program on schools which were regarded as 'high risk'. These were schools in areas where there is a higher incidence of street crime and vandalism. However, the recent attacks on country schools at Broken Hill and West Wyalong have revealed that there is no 'low risk school'.

Electronic surveillance will not eliminate fires and vandalism. It will serve only to reduce the problem. Vandalism will cease only when the perpetrators cease to wish to destroy, or when community attitudes are such that the deterrent is stronger than the will to act.

This does not mean that there is no merit in pursuing a program of electronic surveillance. In fact, there is a wealth of evidence (particularly from Victoria and other States) to suggest that it is an effective means of reducing crime against property in schools. What is important, and what the State Government and the Department of Education both realise, is that electronic surveillance forms an integral part of a wide-reaching program which incorporates a variety of approaches to the task of combating an element in society which causes stress, trauma and economic damage to the community.

Seventy one schools have been connected to the Department's electronic surveillance system. The 1987/88 Security Works Program provides for an additional 125 Secondary, and 125 Primary schools in the Sydney Metropolitan area to be connected to the system. In addition, burglar alarms will be installed in 100 'high risk' country schools. The Department's goal is to connect all schools with security problems to electronic surveillance as soon as practicable.

As a result of the electronic surveillance program, over 120 offenders have been apprehended. This figure includes children currently enrolled in schools, adolescents and professional or potential hardened criminals. The total security program has two main features. Firstly it is a deterrent, and, secondly, it is a means of early detection to prevent serious crime and property damage to school buildings and their contents.

The program also provides for the employment of security guards, including mobile patrols and static guards. A program which provides vacation patrols of schools has been operating for some time, and has proven to be successful. Special security patrols have been organised in areas where vandalism or arson has occurred, and police patrols have assisted in acting as a deterrent to possible perpetrators.

There are several ways in which the improvement of physical security in schools is being approached.

In terms of future and long-term provisions, the design of schools is being carefully investigated to allow 'built in' security measures, and the Schools Building Code incorporates a section for security. Not only is the inclusion of security features in the Schools Building Code advantageous in that present schools can be physically secured more easily, as their design lends itself to this, but, with security an integral part of the school design, it is less evident as 'fortress mentality' for those who live and work in the school environs everyday.

In existing schools, the additions of heavier locks, grilles and bars on windows, the provision of secure stores and, in some cases, perimeter fencing, all assist in making schools more difficult targets.

On a less complicated level, but one which can be of great importance to the security of premises, schools are becoming increasingly conscious of the need to ensure that all precautions are taken, such as storing equipment and records securely at the end of each day, and being vigilant in the locking of doors and windows after school hours. Schools are well aware of such devices as limiting access to certain parts of the school at times when after hours activities are taking place.

Such security is important as a deterrent not only to adolescents, but also to professional burglars who are attracted by expensive specialist equipment readily available in many schools. Fire is sometimes used to camouflage the original crime.

Professional thieves are interested only in readily portable and saleable commodities. One approach in combating their interest in schools as the sources of such products, (which really goes beyond the province of the Department), is a need to curb the ready market in such places as hotels, where contact is made with normally 'honest' citizens, who see the chance for a bargain. A campaign which has been conducted over the past few years to alert people to the criminal responsibility of purchasing such goods needs continued reinforcement if the market, and therefore the thefts, are to be eliminated.

The Minister for Education has expressed support for a supplementary Arson Reward Scheme, paid from State Government funds, to cover schools and other public buildings. It is part of an initiative by the State Government, the Police Department and the Insurance Council of Australia and its aim is to encourage the community to provide information leading to the arrest and conviction of offenders. The scheme will be managed by the Police Department.

Those who work in schools are increasingly aware that they are no longer immune to property crime following the demise of a community ethic which held them apart from such damage through their connection with children and the positive feelings of community ownership. Ultimately, there must be the development

and fostering of an attitude that it is unacceptable to attack
school property, an attitude which seems best developed in areas
where communities regard school buildings as their own, rather
than as belonging to the Government.

The Department recognises the importance of fostering such an
attitude, and of encouraging security consciousness, not just in
students and staff, but in community users of school premises,
such as school Parents and Citizens Associations.

The highly successful Neighbourhood Watch Scheme, which has
promoted co-operation between the community and the NSW Police
Force, has been extended where possible to include schools.
Aside from the benefits derived in terms of prevention or
detection of crime, the scheme has done much to foster awareness
of schools as belonging to, and being an integral part of, a
community, rather than as 'a Government building' which ceases to
be of concern or interest after school hours.

The concept of the Community School Watch Scheme is the voluntary
protection of school property and buildings on a regular roster
basis by members of a Parents and Citizens Association.   The
concept is applicable in circumstances where parents feel that
there is a need for security afforded by parental involvement.
The concept is modelled on several successful systems implemented
at schools. The following is an example of such a scheme.

School Security Watch Program
- John Warby Public School

John Warby Public School is a large first class
primary school located in a vast Housing Commission
development at Airds, Campbelltown, in the
Department of Education's Metropolitan South West
Region. The school has had a history of regular
vandalism and serious breaches of security since
its establishment in 1976. The Principal reports
that 'clean ups' and makeshift repairs had become a
regular feature of Monday mornings and school days
immediately following vacation periods. During the
four school weeks preceding 27 February, sixty
seven windows were broken and on the evening of 27
February the school sustained arson related damage
totalling $100,000.

Following the fire, the Principal and parents
decided to carry out regular evening patrols of the
school premises to prevent any further such attacks
on the school. The group of interested parents

grew in number and eventually their role was formalised under the auspices of the P & C Association as a school voluntary watch program.

The Watch Program involves fourteen fathers who patrol the school premises on a rostered basis each evening and all day Saturday and Sunday. The group is equipped with walkie talkie radios and is linked to a citizens' emergency radio service known as CREST. This enables them to communicate promptly with police and other emergency services as required.

Since the establishment of the voluntary watch program, the incidence of vandalism and breaches of security sustained by the school has been reduced to just one broken window and minor damage to two external security lights since February.

The Principal, parents and staff are delighted with these outstanding results. Staff morale and school/community relations have been strengthened enormously, and the school's vandalism bill almost totally eliminated.

The Director, Metropolitan South West Region, is presently promoting watch programs in other affected schools throughout the Region and is hopeful of achieving similar positive results.

It is important for the scheme that a high profile is maintained, that details of the roster are publicised amongst students and the local media, that nearby citizens are informed, and that locals in the vicinity are encouraged to report suspicious movements.

Ministerial approval is required to establish the scheme in a school, and there are a number of criteria which must be met before such approval will be given. The Department of Education insists that:

i)   there should be passive surveillance only;

ii)   volunteer patrols should not accost people;

iii) volunteer patrols should report any detections to the police, who will take the necessary action;

iv)   the school should advertise that volunteer patrols are operating;

42

v)   volunteers must not place themselves in a 'risk'
       situation;

vi)   the Department of Education will not be involved in
       arranging or meeting premium costs for insurance cover.

A small number of schools have adopted this scheme successfully,
however, there is some concern expressed by members of the
community anxious to avoid fostering vigilante style behaviour,
or worried at the implications of the level of risk to which
members of such patrols may be subjected, simply by choosing to
be part of the roster. Such concerns have been considered by the
Department, and it is felt that the regulations set out should
minimise any possibility of Community School Watch groups
providing anything but a positive contribution to monitoring,
particularly the physical security of school premises through
observation of any suspicious movements. Much of the success of
the scheme lies in the deterrent effect of the publicity
surrounding it.

JOINT AGENCY PREVENTIVE ACTION

Generally the Department is seeking to promote co-operation
between the Police, the community, the fire authorities and the
Public Works Department to devise measures to minimise the
incidence of school vandalism and arson. Importantly, the
Department seeks and encourages the assistance of school staff,
students, parents and the community in alerting the authorities
whenever there is a likelihood of a school being vandalised. To
promote such co-operation requires education and the building of
trust and good communication between all those involved.

A pilot project entitled, School – Community Educational Awareness Security Program is to operate in 1988, at a cost of
$130,000. It is a response to the view that the Department of
Education is entirely responsible for combating the serious
social problem of crime in schools, and will operate in the
Metropolitan South West Region (an area incorporating a number of
'high risk' suburbs of Sydney), under the authority and auspices
of the Schools Directorate, and overseen by a specially appointed
committee. The committee will include representatives from the
Department of Education (Schools Directorate, Properties
Directorate and the Region) and the Police Department.

The Police report that the proposal has been very well received
by the Counter Arson Committee, and that there is enthusiasm for
a project with the aim of trialling a variety of methods to
offset arson, vandalism and illegal entry in a high security risk
region, in order to develop an operational model which could then
be applied in other Regions of the State as required.

In a trial project such as this, selection of staff is important, as the success of the project will rest principally on the quality of the personnel. The list of qualities needed by Education personnel is extensive, and it is worthwhile examining this, as it sheds light on the human resources necessary to ensure that prevention of crime against property in schools goes beyond providing physical barriers to would-be perpetrators, and towards instilling a sense of community responsibility.

Officers working in the Program will require: initiative and drive; expertise in inter-personal communication skills with both children and adults; the capacity for self-direction; ability to design and implement teaching modules; tact and diplomacy in work with police units; regional and school staffs and the community (at times in sensitive circumstances following arson or vandalism attacks); the ability to respond to variable working conditions such as evening attendance at community meetings; and possibly some weekend commitments, and experience in counselling.

RESEARCH INTO SCHOOL PROPERTY CRIME

It is important in the research of crime in schools to gather, analyse and interpret statistics. There are two types of vandalism which occur in schools:

1.   vandalism from within the school (often occurring during school hours, as well as after hours), and

2.   vandalism from without (usually occurring after school hours, and frequently by perpetrators unconnected to that particular school).

For the first there is a need to determine the cause of this and the motive behind the actions, and then look to possible solutions and means of preventing these occurrences. For the second, the methods developed by the Education Department are aimed at addressing the problem. In both of these areas there is a need to determine where responsibility lies, but, rather than simply apportioning blame, to then address the problem through education, as well as by providing physical security.

In an attempt to address these questions, a research study is to be conducted by the NSW Bureau of Crime Statistics and Research into school vandalism and arson. The unrestricted study is to include investigation into the following areas:

a)   why school students, alone of all the clients of public facilities, feel compelled to burn and wreck those facilities;

b)   what pleasure or fulfilment such arsonists derive from
        their actions;

c)   what is their motivation;

d)   to what extent is it suppressed revenge against an
        incident at school or general alienation at the school;

e)   to what extent media publicity breeds the idea in the
        minds of some children that vandalism is a way to
        achieve notoriety or some other need?

In regard to this last point, the media is an important tool in
the fight against property crime in schools, yet there is the
risk that it can, by providing the wrong impression of such
crime, promote in certain people the concept of achieving
notoriety through 'newsworthy' events. In an article in the
Sydney Morning Herald on 14 August 1987, discussing the need for
improved security in NSW schools, it was stated that:

        The Department is right when it points to
        sensationalist reports in the media as the
        catalyst often for a spate of arson attempts.

In fact, the journalist who wrote the article has noted a salient
point - that is is 'sensationalist reports' that may offer
encouragement to potential vandals and arsonists. Responsible
journalism can do much to further the Department's cause,
particularly in the area of alerting the community as a whole to
the extent of the problem.

A PREVENTIVE MEDIA CAMPAIGN

It was with this last point in mind that the Department arranged
a radio campaign to draw attention to the problem.

The campaign was aimed at mature people with the intent of
developing a type of unstructured neighbourhood watch on school
buildings. The message of the campaign was that schools are
community buildings paid for by taxpayers, and as such, they
should be protected by the community. People who live near
schools were urged to report to Police any suspicious activity in
or near school buildings. It was believed that such action might
prevent damage to schools - damage which must be paid for by the
taxpayers.

The campaign was targeted towards people living in the western an
south western parts of the Sydney Metropolitan area. Four
commercial ratio stations were chosen to broadcast 30 second

commercials for 26 weeks, beginning on 9 June 1987. The following is a sample script from the campaign comprising sound effects (SFX) and an announcer (ANNR):

MUSIC: 'Boys and girls come out to play'.

SFX: (Vandals smashing a classroom)

ANNR: Every once in a while the gang gets together to play at the school.

SFX: (Glass being broken)

ANNR: They have a smashing time.

SFX: (Hear kids laughing and generally being loathsome)

ANNR: It's great fun for them and they get their kicks for free. But as a taxpayer it costs you sixteen million dollars a year.

SFX: (Hear flames)

ANNR: The money they waste through their vandalism could build two new high schools or five new primary schools a year.

SFX: (More smashing)

ANNR: If you live near a school ... be a spoil sport ... the next time the gang gets together and wrecks a school ... call the Police ... quick as you can.

This is an urgent SOS. Save our Schools ...

SFX: (Fade out effects)

ANNR: ... from vandals.

An evaluation of the success of this campaign is taking place, but present indications are that it has served to heighten community awareness of the problems of arson and vandalism in schools.

Throughout the period in which arson and vandalism in schools has grown to be a major problem, the mass media has focused a great deal of attention on the matter, and several general comments can be made concerning the media and reporting of crime in schools:

Firstly, there is frequently a tendency to focus the report towards lack of Departmental action in addressing the problem, and to apportion blame to deficiencies in the education system generally. In terms of community awareness, reports which focus on the loss felt by other students, and the disruption caused to their education over an extended period of time have the desired effect of 'humanising' the event away from the destruction of a Government ('theirs') rather than a Community ('ours') facility.

Secondly, unless 'sensational', reports of the apprehension of offenders are often less prominent than reports of the destruction. While the cost of the damage in dollars is reported, familiarity with the event (no media fault here) makes it easy for people to dismiss the amount of taxpayers' money that vandals and arsonists (usually children and adolescents) are squandering.

Thirdly, while using all possible means of heightening community awareness of the problems in our schools, with a view to encouraging participation in their prevention, communities are only really likely to feel a sense of attachment or interest in schools if they know of the good things that are happening in them, both from within the school and from Regional and Departmental initiatives. Positive reporting of activities in schools goes a long way to establishing them as objects of value in the community.

In this sense, the Department's encouragement of joint school/community facilities goes a long way to both fostering a sense of community commitment and to countering the likelihood of vulnerability to come. As the press article quoted above goes on to say:

> It (the Department) has a valid point when it claims that schools are peculiarly vulnerable to vandals. Unlike other major public institutions, such as hospitals, they are empty for long periods, and they are easily broken into. For disgruntled students or troublemakers, schools are an obvious target as the front line of an authority they hate.
>
> (Sydney Morning Herald, 14 August 1987)

CONCLUSION

The Department's encouragement of community use of schools is a further means of improving security in schools. The Department is also aware that there are curriculum implications in devising means by which arson and vandalism can be prevented in schools.

The importance of maintaining the idea that schools are warm, caring places lies also in the teaching of self-discipline and values in children. Those involved in education place great store in the provision and maintenance of a secure environment for their students - secure in both the physical and emotional sense, in as far as the school has the power to provide this. Parents, quite reasonably, believe and expect that this security is provided, and expect that their children will be educated within a setting which is free from violence or the threat of violence.

Many of these people would probably not consider that the vandalism and arson which occurs in schools is a violation of this expectation, since the aftermath of property crime is usually fiscal or emotional rather than actually physically harmful to the child, yet vandalism and arson are surely acts of violence. Children need to be made more aware of this fact, as well as of the long-term consequences of such action. Peer support, or lack thereof, is often the greatest determining factor in student action. Of course, it would be simplistic to believe that all possible offenders, and particularly those for whom alienation is the cause of their aggression, are going to be deterred because they know that others disapprove, however, if it was seen before damage was done that the overwhelming feeling among their peers was to condemn such action, then many would probably reconsider.

Security should also be seen as part of the learning process of responsibility. There are excellent opportunities to promote these attitudes within such areas as peer support programs and classroom discussion. The Department is actively engaged in promoting research and action which can bring about education in this matter through curriculum planning.

This discussion covers a number of initiatives in which the State Government and the Department of Education are engaged in the formulation of an approach to prevent criminal damage in schools. The individual components range from physical security (locks, grilles, etc), detection and warning devices (electronic surveillance system, alarms), human involvement in physical security (guards, Community and Neighbourhood Watch Schemes), to media campaigns and research programs. There is, coupled to all these measures, the underlying approach to making the whole community, both inside and outside schools, aware of what is happening and of the need to prevent the promulgation of the idea that vandalism and arson are unfortunate problems of society that have to be lived with until 'the Government' does something about them.

There is evidence to show that the approaches taken to combat property crime in NSW schools are working, with a drop in the number of fires in the July-October figure of 1987 (35 fires) compared with the same period in 1986 (45 fires).

The main thrust of the security program in schools is seen to be the connection of schools to electronic surveillance, and there is evidence to show that the measures being taken are achieving good results. Electronic surveillance, however, has its limitations and, as observers of crime will readily note, as one opening is closed another appears.

It is not the intention of the Department to continue to strengthen and fortify schools, as this would have most serious consequences, not the least on the morale of school communities. The alternative to fortification is the development of positive attitudes in the community, and the Department is pursuing a number of programs designed to prevent property crime in schools at the source, by teaching community awareness and fostering a sense of pride in ownership in schools.

* * * * * *

DISCUSSION

Q: You pointed out that you were keen to encourage community involvement to watch over schools. Couldn't the money being spent on electronics, apprehension and prosecution be better spent to that end?

Allsopp: It is the Government that decides what action to take. Electronics are seen as a valuable deterrent and a way of detecting offenders in the act and reducing the damage they may cause.

Q: Catholic schools seem to suffer less vandalism. Why do you think that is so?

Allsopp: I think because those schools select their own students and often have fairly strict rules about behaviour. But, in addition, there is usually a church and often teachers' accommodation nearby.

Q: In days gone by, schools always had fences around them and the problem did not seem so great. Should we try that again?

Allsopp: We do have fences and electronics in some schools but that is generally seen as a last resort. We would have to seek the views of the local community about a school fence because that could, for instance, cause property values to fall.

Q: Do other educational institutions, for example, TAFE colleges, also suffer in what are your worst areas?

Allsopp: I'm not sure.

Q: Why has it taken so long to react to the problem and spend the big money that's necessary?

Allsopp: As the costs of repairing damage or replacing facilities increases, the cost of preventive action becomes relatively less.

NEIGHBOURHOOD WATCH: A DISCUSSION

Neighbourhood Watch programs have become increasingly common throughout Australia in recent years. Their contribution to crime prevention was considered at the seminar through discussion following the introduction of some research undertaken at the Institute.

That research by Dr Satyanshu Mukherjee and Dr Paul Wilson had been published as Number 8 in the Institute's Trends and Issues Series the week prior to the seminar. Entitled 'Neighbourhood Watch: Issues and Policy Implications', the research was described to seminar participants by Dr Wilson as a preliminary retrospective assessment of Victoria's neighbourhood watch program rather than an on-going planned evaluation requiring specially collected data. The following extracts from the Trends and Issues report outline the research discussed at the seminar by its authors:

* * * * * *

ISSUES AND POLICY IMPLICATIONS

Paul Wilson
and Satyanshu Mukherjee
Australian Institute of Criminology

'In this report we raise issues relating to the neighbourhood watch program with the object of sensitising policy makers, criminal justice administrators, and researchers to the need for systematic research and the development of data bases for 'watch' programs. Victoria has been selected for analysis because the anti-crime program discussed in this report is well developed there and also because of the distinctive nature of its neighbourhood watch program.....

WHAT IS COMMUNITY CRIME PREVENTION?

Citizens tend to believe that crime prevention is the task solely of the police and other criminal justice agencies and that crimes occur because of the failure of these agencies. Such a belief exists partly because of the impression created by official agencies and partly because of ignorance. The demands by police for more personnel and their calls for increased powers in the face of rising crime generate a strong impression to the public that these steps are needed to check crime. Yet, historically, members of the community looked after the safety of local areas and it was only when modern police emerged in the early nineteenth century that law enforcement agencies took over a task formerly undertaken by citizens.

The most important element of community crime prevention appears to bring about social interaction, whereby residents of the community maintain a degree of familiarity with each other. Such interaction and familiarity should, in theory at lest, make it possible to detect strangers in the community. And finally, crime prevention theory suggests that such interactions may lead to a cohesive neighbourhood. The basic philosophy of community crime prevention is that social interaction and citizen familiarity can play an important role in preventing, detecting, and reporting criminal behaviour.

The neighbourhood watch program is one of many types of community crime prevention activities. A major thrust of watch programs is to reduce opportunity for crime. This task is carried out by improving citizens' awareness about public safety, by improving residents' attitudes and behaviour in reporting crime and suspicious events in the neighbourhood and by reducing vulnerability to crime with the help of property identification and installation of effective security devices. The individual watch programs within a state or district may vary in emphasis and organisational context.....

While there is no doubt that there was initially a substantial drop in residential burglaries in Victoria and in other states, questions remain as to whether this drop is due directly to neighbourhood watch or to other factors such as new police patrolling methods, citizen consciousness being raised by media attention independent of neighbourhood watch programs or changes in the general economic climate.

The Victoria Police themselves are cautious in ascribing reductions in burglary rates entirely to neighbourhood watch programs. They note that, while they do not attribute all of the reduction to neighbourhood watch, the program has been the only significant change in policing strategy in recent times and therefore is certainly part of the reason for such significant reductions.....

NEIGHBOURHOOD WATCH AND THE DISPLACEMENT EFFECT

Changes in the incidence of crime as a consequence of neighbour-hood watch is referred to as displacement of crime and this denotes a redistribution rather than reduction in crime. Displacement can occur in several ways. A 'successful' anti-crime program may result in changes in criminal behaviour. Offenders, by circumventing preventive measures, may move to other neighbourhoods where no such schemes are in operation,

select different targets, use different methods or change the
time of committing burglaries, or engage in other offence types,
etc. What follows in the remaining part of this section is a
preliminary attempt to examine this issue.....

(Hereafter followed a 'preliminary attempt' to examine this issue
It involved consideration of the percentage changes in rates of
residential burglary, non residential burglary, motor vehicle
theft and 'other' theft in each of Victoria's 23 police
districts.)

The 23 police districts, in terms of watch content, can be divide
into four groups: districts with no neighbourhood watch, those
with population coverage of under 16 per cent (low intervention),
districts with 16 to 30 per cent coverage (medium intervention),
and districts with a coverage of over 30 per cent (high
intervention).

Looking at the impact on residential burglary, it is quite clear
that all the four high intervention districts and only one medium
intervention district produced good results in reducing
residential burglaries. Thus, they lend very reasonable support
to the objective of neighbourhood watch in suppressing
residential burglary.

Three of the high intervention districts also showed good results
in reducing non-residential burglaries. The district with the
highest concentration of neighbourhood watch also attained
significant reduction in motor vehicle thefts. On the negative
side, in one high intervention district, non-residential burglary
increased significantly, and in two other districts 'other'
thefts jumped sharply. These figures tend to suggest that the
expansion of neighbourhood watch will attain desirable results in
reducing residential burglaries, but the impact of such schemes
on other property crimes is unclear.....

NON-CRIME PREVENTION FUNCTIONS OF NEIGHBOURHOOD WATCH

It is possible that future research might establish that though
neighbourhood watch programs do reduce rates of burglary,
displacement effects occur so that, for example, auto theft
concurrently increases. Even if this result is found in
subsequent evaluation research, it does not mean that this form
of community crime prevention is a failure......there may be
advantages associated with neighbourhood watch programs not
related to reductions in specific crime activities in residential
areas. The following assertions, for example, have been made
regarding the benefits of neighbourhood watch programs.

Individuals, often previously isolated and unknown to each other,
form social relations as a result of neighbourhood watch programs
and activities. Increased interaction between residents assists
in breathing life into neighbourhoods marked previously by
alienation and community apathy.

The police and the public, previously suspicious and distant from each other, are able to interact in productive and creative ways. As a result of these positive interactions, police/public relations markedly improve.

The police, who often interact with the public in conflict situations (serving summonses, charging persons, booking motorists, etc) tend often to become overly cynical and mistrustful of the public. The formation, implementation and maintenance of neighbourhood watch programs may well reorientate the attitude of officers towards citizens in a more constructive and positive direction.

Fear and anxiety associated with worrying about crime may decrease. As a result of realising that surveillance measures are operating within a neighbourhood, residents are more willing to walk the streets, interact with their neighbours and leave their house for social activities. Neighbourhood watch will, in short, reduce the fear and anxiety associated with crime even if the actual level of crime remains the same.

Neighbourhood watch activities can be generalised into other constructive community initiatives such as improving road and traffic conditions, child minding networks, commuter-transport sharing and so on.

However, for each of these assertions counter-arguments can be mounted. For example, it is possible to argue that increased community activity as a result of a neighbourhood watch program may lead to increased fear of crime.

CONCLUSIONS

On balance, it would appear that community crime prevention, in the form of neighbourhood watch, has some redeeming values. Although it is realised that the official crime statistics are no the best set of data for evaluation, decreases in recorded numbers of residential burglaries in some neighbourhood watch areas cannot be overlooked. There remain, however, many nagging issues; establishing causal links between neighbourhood watch and crime reduction and displacement effects are but two of these which need to be examined more fully. Examination of these issues is by no means an easy task as there appear to be numerous conceptual and methodological impediments. A few of the important obstacles are summarised below and it is hoped that systematic evaluation of neighbourhood watch programs in Australia, will grapple with these and other obstacles.

PRODUCING SOCIAL COHESION

It has been pointed out that an important element of a community crime prevention program is to bring about social cohesion. During the past few decades, the ever changing life style of

urban centres has resulted in almost complete erosion of informal
social interaction. Can a program with a single objective of
reducing residential burglary reverse this complex social trend?

DEFINING NEIGHBOURHOOD WATCH

The operation of neighbourhood watch incorporates many
activities and each activity can vary in content. This means
that the definition of a program has to define the activities
involved fairly specifically. For example, public education
programs, informal surveillance by residents, increase in police
patrols, marking of property, increased use of security devices,
improved methods of burglary investigation, and so on, are some
of the activities which constitute a watch program. Yet, since
it is possible for each of these activities to be carried out in
more than one way, each should be properly classified.

TARGETING ANTI-CRIME MEASURES

Research and statistical evidence indicate socio-economically
disadvantaged areas have high crime rates. It is not
sufficiently clear whether these areas receive priority for crime
prevention efforts. Significant reduction in crime may not be
possible unless interventions are operative in high crime areas.

DESCRIBING ORGANISATIONAL ELEMENTS

It is important that the method of selection and characteristics
of committee members, the structure of the committee, its
relationship with the local police and many other organisational
matters be described in sufficient detail. It is also necessary
to monitor changes in the organisational element over time.

MEASURING UNINTENDED OUTCOMES

Crime reduction and not redistribution is the goal of anti-crime
measures. Careful attention needs, therefore, to be given to
assessing the displacement effects, if any.

ELIMINATING ROOT CAUSES OF CRIME

Success of neighbourhood watch in reducing residential crime and
fear of crime is not the end of the story. The public must also
consider action programs targeted at the root causes of crime.
For example, criminological research demonstrates that youngsters
are disproportionately represented in illegal activity. Research
also shows that much of the criminogenic process is linked to the
development stages of the youth. Improving educational, employment, health and recreational opportunities available to the
youth would seem, therefore, to be of paramount significance.

To conclude: we believe that although neighbourhood watch programs offer considerable promise as a method of reducing certain crimes, the schemes should not be adopted uncritically. Preliminary evidence suggests that the effectiveness of such schemes may dissipate over time and that displacement effects can occur. What are badly needed, in the Australian context, are system evaluations of both the process and outcome of implementing neighbourhood watch programs.'

* * * * * *

Sergeant Chris Coster, the Co-ordinator of Neighbourhood Watch programs in Victoria, responded vigorously to the research just described. His main concern centred on the fact that the study had not been a prospective solidly planned evaluation (a fact acknowledged by Dr Wilson) and the final conclusions neither resulted directly from the research into the Victorian program nor fairly reflected the positive features of that program. The researchers responded in turn to Sergeant Coster's criticism, but that detailed discussion is not reproduced here. Rather, a paper by Sergeant Coster, outlining his recent visit to North America to examine existing programs, which was distributed to seminar participants, is reproduced below.

* * * * * *

NEIGHBOURHOOD WATCH IN AMERICA

Chris Coster
Victoria Police

My recent Churchill Fellowship study tour took me to Los Angeles, San Francisco, Sacramento, Seattle, Minneapolis, Chicago, Detroit, Toronto, Ottawa, Montreal, New York, Washington DC, and Houston, to look at Neighbourhood Watch and other crime prevention programs in those places.

Everyone believes when it comes to crime, the Americans beat everyone. Unfortunately, that is not the reality. There is only one city in the United States that has a higher burglary level than us, that is New York, and they don't beat us by much. The general facts are that in 1985 Australia had a burglary rate per head of population 35.68 per cent higher than the United States. Just five years earlier, in 1980, the United States was 28.96 per cent higher than Australia.

So what was the factor that made America's burglary level so low in comparison to ours? For American Police Officers, the answer was simple, they all put it down to the effect that Neighbourhood

Watch has had. But I didn't think that was the total answer. Americans have a completely different attitude to crime compared with most Australians. When they leave their homes, they expect to be broken into and therefore it has become automatic for them to take the necessary precautions. People generally recognise and understand their role in crime prevention better than people do here. So the end result is that Neighbourhood Watch and associated burglary prevention programs have simply become a part of everyday life. It never even makes the news to any degree.

IMPROVING NEIGHBOURHOOD WATCH

My first recommendation is that Neighbourhood Watch programs should work to modify the attitudes of people. Neighbourhood Watch leaders have a responsibility to make people aware of the problem they are facing.

My next recommendation is, paradoxically, to always think small. Quite obviously we have a structure that can and is working extremely well. It is quite clear the most important level in this organisation is the Zone Leader. If Zone Leaders are constantly liaising with residents of their zones, then Neighbourhood Watch will be strong and be maintained into the 21st Century. However, people get things done best in groups of no larger than 30 and preferably fewer, so the local zone and its leader comprise the important basis for the Neighbourhood Watch program.

My last recommendation is diversification. Most Neighbourhood Watch programs I studied spoke of the need to diversify their activities beyond crime alone. This seems to be a very important issue in maintaining interest. A National Crime Prevention Council study on maintaining Neighbourhood Watch programs features a quote, 'PROGRAMS SHOULD FOCUS ON CRIME AND GENERAL NEIGHBOURHOOD PROBLEMS'. The message is quite clear: while the crime issue may have convinced citizens to join, it is usually not enough to maintain interest.

I have often said that you must examine why people got involved with Neighbourhood Watch to start with. There are three usual reasons, firstly, a desire to liaise more closely with the local police; secondly, a desire to reduce crime; and thirdly, a desire to improve their quality of life. The improvement of quality of life will not necessarily be achieved through crime reduction alone. Quite clearly the American experience is that people should be concerned with any issue that affects their neighbourhood, and that Neighbourhood Watch is an excellent forum for addressing any problems they have.

One Police Officer in Los Angeles explained it this way. He said, 'If McDonalds only sold Big Macs, their impact on the fast food market would have obvious limitations, but by diversifying their product range, they expand their impact and profits'. By diversifying, your profits will be fewer crimes. I suggest to you that by encouraging people to use Neighbourhood Watch as a forum for solving any community problem while maintaining burglary prevention as your primary target, you will have a strong, vibrant Neighbourhood Watch program and satisfy all three needs people have when they become a part of this program.

OVERSEAS STRATEGIES

The major thrust of my study was to find specific strategies to ensure maintenance of Neighbourhood Watch. I will now give you a short explanation of each of the major strategies I identified. Whilst remembering my comments about thinking small, every Neighbourhood Watch program I saw emphasised the importance of having block maps. The idea is that each block captain, or Zone Leader in our case, put together a block map identifying the number of each house, the name of the occupants, their phone number and many of them include a generalised profile in the form of usual cars that will be at the house or expected to visit.

There are several advantages to this strategy. For example, when a person is reporting a suspicious incident, they are able to refer to their block map and instead of saying, well its three houses down from me on the other side of the road, they can actually identify the house number. Residents are also able to quickly identify any cars that aren't usually outside the house and whilst there may not be enough suspicion to report the incident, they can at least take a note of the registration number. It also means that each person in the block actually knows the name of the person living in each house and it removes to a degree that suburban anonymity. This is an activity Zone Leaders can implement immediately and then update their zone map as the need arises. If a person doesn't wish to have their name on the map, then a space is left and that person doesn't get a map. There shouldn't be any pressure on people to include their name, it is a matter of choice and to their benefit, but if some people don't want to be included, they shouldn't be forced.

Operation Cleansweep

In many neighbourhoods the introduction of a program called Operation Cleansweep had a very positive effect on further bringing people together. Operation Cleansweep works by neighbourhoods periodically - usually every six or twelve months - holding a beautification day or weekend. Once again, there was no compulsion on people to participate, but once the initiative was used, pride in the neighbourhood increased and

again, the people were brought closer together. The experience
is that once people redevelop their pride in the neighbourhood,
they are more likely to do the necessary things to prevent crime
and take the necessary action to report suspicious activity.
I was most impressed with this particular strategy because
several studies in the United States of America have shown that
properties indicating the occupants look after them have a lower
risk of burglary than obviously unkempt premises. The same
applies for neighbourhoods.

McGruff

In most cities throughout the USA, a national crime prevention
mascot has been adopted. The mascot is a dog called McGruff the
crime dog. I was aware of McGruff before the trip and didn't
think the idea was very good. It was my opinion that having a
dog as a crime prevention mascot tended to trivialise a serious
issue. However, my opinion changed dramatically. The recognition rate of McGruff is incredibly high, and it now serves
as a focus for all crime prevention initiatives. I believe we
need a similar feature that can be quickly recognised and
associated with a whole range of crime prevention operations.

National Night Out

The next highly successful program used by Neighbourhood Watch is
called National Night Out. Some of you will have seen this
featured on the NBC Today show on Channel 7. The idea is that
people go out of their house on one night in the year right
across the nation, they put the front light on and meet with the
neighbours. It has been highly successful in bringing people
back together as a neighbourhood. I asked if there were any
other benefits apart from the community cohesion it may develop.
The reply was that National Night Out is also a symbolic
statement of literally millions of people reclaiming their
neighbourhood. Reclaiming their neighbourhood from criminal
intrusion, although the risk of their home being broken into is
less than ours. I am sure that with a little co-operation, a
similar operation could be implemented here.

Computer Technology

Many police Departments have now purchased, in association with
Neighbourhood Watch programs, computers with communication
capability to residents of Neighbourhood Watch areas. The way it
works is that if, for example, the police need to get a phone
message to every resident in any particular area, they simply put
a message into the computer and then give the computer
instructions on when to call and how many times to try if it
doesn't answer, and when to stop making calls. The whole
operation can be set up in two minutes. Essentially, it is a
computer aided phone tree.

I was most impressed with these systems, their versatility is exceptional. Currently they are used by detectives to eliminate the need for house to house enquiries. They are used by crime prevention officers to put out crime prevention messages. Crime alerts are put out by crime analysts after identification of a particular problem in an area.

The system is nothing short of brilliant. Just imagine the applications. For example, the recent tragedy in Clifton Hill. As soon as that situation was known, a person could have put a message on the computer to call each house in that area, telling them to remain in their homes. When the incident finished, a message could then have been dispatched asking people to check their back yards for any evidence that could have been dumped. The phone calls to each resident could have started within two minutes of appraisal of the seriousness of the situation.

I believe this is an area we can improve substantially. I am confident we could implement such a system, which would have a significant impact. Whilst talking about computer technology some of you will have heard recent press reports by civil libertarians condemning a proposed phone service which could tell you who is calling before you answer, or at the very least identify where the call is being made from when the phone is answered. Every police department I visited had an enhanced 911 system in place, it meant that as soon as the Communications Centre answered the phone, a VDU displayed the address the call was coming from and the subscriber for that number. The information, together with the incident report, would then be switched to in-car computers to available police. Often these calls would go out without a word being spoken. We certainly have a long way to go in that area.

Recognition

Recognition of achievement was considered to be almost the most important issue of all in maintaining Neighbourhood Watch. All departments have awards of various types for civilians involved with Neighbourhood Watch. The Victorian State Committee is researching this area, and will make recommendations soon, but it's an area worth acting upon.

Crime Analysis

Crime analysis is also a vital area. This was summed up most succinctly by a Sergeant from the Los Angeles Sheriff's Department who said, 'How can you expect to prevent crime if you don't know where it is happening?' We have spoken many times in the past about the importance of crime analysis on a local level. Area Co-ordinator training sessions spend a considerable amount of time on the subject. In America, many departments are now combining their crime prevention units with their crime analysis sections.

Undoubtedly in the past two years the most significant change in American policing has been the dedication to knowing more about crime patterns and the use of the information in their crime prevention programs. Neighbourhood Watch areas, to achieve maximum impact must devote more of their time to aggressively analysing what is happening in their areas and then doing something about it.

POSITIVE INTERACTION

The most critical factor we face today is maintaining Neighbour-hood Watch. In Montreal, Canada, and Houston, Texas, they have implemented programs into Neighbourhood Watch aimed at ensuring Police have all available information about any problems in neighbourhoods. The best of the two was in Houston.

The system there is that representatives of each Neighbourhood Watch area meet monthly on a district basis, with the Lieutenant (equivalent to a Senior Sergeant) from the local precinct. The program is called the Positive Interaction Program. The purpose of the Lieutenant's presence is to receive information about any problems that have come from the individual areas. There is no restriction on the types of problems raised. The duty of the Lieutenant is to then explain whether the complaint is a police matter or otherwise, and if it's not, to refer the person to the appropriate authority. If it is a police matter, then he will get details of it, task his men to the problem and report results at the next meeting.

The Police Chief in Houston explained it is a reversal of usual Neighbourhood Watch philosophy in that the reason for police attendance is to receive information, and not to give it. The advantage from his point of view is that Police can then operate with all the available information, not just that which is reported as a crime. This system has been an unqualified success. It ensures maintenance by giving people an opportunity to have an input into local policing, it improves the productivity of police by tasking them to identified community problems. It also improves the attitude of police to crime prevention because, firstly, if they don't take action, it's the Lieutenant who will be embarrassed at the next meeting and, secondly, their relationship with the people is improved because people now see them as their police force. I am absolutely convinced that the single most important thing we can do to ensure the maintenance of Neighbourhood Watch is to follow this line of thinking. After talking with several Lieutenants in Houston, I am convinced we must do more to involve Officers in

Charge of Police Stations in community consultation. Community consultation in this context is not groups of civilians trying to direct police activities, it is simply developing a forum for civilians to improve their communications with the police.

The system in Montreal is similar, except they go further and have only been going for a short time. They have divided sub-districts into small areas of up to 100 homes and nominated a police officer to that area. The police officer will still carry out his usual duties except that he has a responsibility to visit each of those households at least once every years, and ask them what concerns they have in the neighbourhood. Once again, the Officers in Charge of the stations are the focal point because they then have to prepare daily tasking sheets including identified community problems.

I believe this issue is the single factor that will determine the longevity of Neighbourhood Watch. For us there are two responsibilities. The first is for Zone Leaders to maintain contact with the residents of each zone so they can report community problems which do not amount to an actual crime and pass on this information through the various meetings. The second is for police to expand their role to not only giving information about crime, but to receive information and act on it. I think the success of this type of initiative depends on the involvement of Officers in Charge of Stations. For that reason, the first task I intend to undertake to improve Neighbourhood Watch is to plan the logistics of involving Officers in Charge of Stations and then to make appropriate recommendations to the department.

SUMMARY

In summary, Neighbourhood Watch in the USA and Canada is aimed at burglary prevention and community cohesion. Many people speak in terms of 'reclaiming' their neighbourhood. Fortunately, I don't think we have reached the stage where we have to 'reclaim' our neighbourhoods, I hope crime never gets that bad in this country. However, it could happen, and I assure you it is much more difficult to reclaim a neighbourhood than it is to prevent a neighbourhood degenerating to such a stage. That theme is reinforced by the Executive Director of the USA National Crime Prevention Council, Mr Jack Calhoun, who wrote in his 1986 Annual Report, 'Crime Prevention must show individuals how to protect themselves, it must also strengthen our communities.'

* * * * * *

Before general discussion about Neighbourhood Watch, commentaries were invited from two participants from different fields. Mr Andrew Hiller provided an academic's view and Mr John Westbury spoke from the perspective of the Insurance industry.

Mr Hiller distributed copies of some of his own work on Neighbourhood Watch and community policing and provided the following comments:

*   *   *   *   *   *

NEIGHBOURHOOD WATCH, THE ELDERLY AND ETHNIC COMMUNITIES

Andrew Hiller
University of Queensland

Various developments in community policing, are in my view related to the development, operation or effectiveness of Neighbourhood Watch schemes.

Thus the development of networks of District Community Relations Officers and District Community Liaison Officers provides experienced police community relations officers at District level to co-ordinate and otherwise assist in Neighbourhood Watch programs. The same point applies generally to Police Community Relations Bureau and Police Community Relations Branches and their personnel, including their capacity to aid both other police and concerned citizens in implementing such programs.

Particular note should be taken of senior citizens and of the valuable contribution they can make to Neighbourhood Watch programs and towards crime prevention generally, including assistance to other senior citizens.

The area of crime prevention for senior citizens is particularly relevant, as many senior citizens spend a lot of time at home and are in a good position to observe what is going on about them. Interested members of this section of the community - and no doubt there would be several - can play an invaluable role in Neighbourhood Watch programs and towards reduction of property crime generally, as well as with respect to reducing other offences in their neighbourhood. Further, senior citizen residents who participate in Neighbourhood Watch programs are in a good position to influence other senior citizens as to the importance of reducing the opportunities for crime, both against their person and property, by taking recommended precautions, as well as by having good liaison with other residents in their neighbourhood, with senior citizen groups and with local police. Good liaison with ethnic groups and organisations and relevant State Government bodies should also be kept in mind, particularly in areas containing an appreciable number of recently arrived or elderly immigrants.

The field of ethnic liaison has implications for Neighbourhood Watch. Police ethnic liaison officers are in a good position to publicise Neighbourhood Watch programs through addresses to Ethnic Communities' Councils, ethnic groups and other appropriate bodies. In States where Ethnic Affairs Commissions exist, as in New South Wales, Victoria, South Australia and Western Australia, police can seek their support in promoting an understanding of the concept of Neighbourhood Watch. In Queensland, the relevant State Government body is the office of the Director of Ethnic Affairs, in the Department of Family and Youth Services which comes under the portfolio of the Minister for Family Services, Youth and Ethnic Affairs. Appropriate literature in both the English language and other languages can be distributed with the assistance of Ethnic Communities' Councils, Ethnic Affairs Commissions and other like bodies. Such literature has already been issued by police in some States, eg by the New South Wales Police Community Relations Bureau, in a variety of languages, with the support of some insurance companies.

The importance of obtaining and using media publicity at State-wide as well as at local level, requires no further comment.

On the international horizon, it is interesting to note that the British Home Secretary, Mr Douglas Hurd, in the House of Commons in May, 1987, stated that there were 29,500 Neighbourhood Watch Schemes in England and Wales. Whereas three years ago there were only about 1,000. He described the increase as amazing and encouraging and noted that there had been a real outburst of energy by the citizen in collaboration with the police. He assured the House that these schemes would be promoted further.

* * * * * *

SOCIETY'S ATTITUDE TO CRIME

John Westbury
Insurance Council of Australia

The raison d'etre for the birth of insurance companies was to provide security for policyholders against unforeseeable disaster. Insurers accept a relationship of good faith with all those who take out an insurance policy. If policyholders are able to present a reasonable case then insurers will honour the contract. Simultaneously, they are adamant that the public must harness its potential to stamp out crime by being alert and responsible. A productive relationship between both parties is based on mutual co-operation and respect. Neighbourhood Watch schemes epitomise the effective of joint community action against crime.

Hopefully neighbourhood watch programs may change people's behaviour and make them more careful concerning safeguarding their own property. Carelessness is a continuing and worrying problem for insurance companies.

Unlocked doors and windows, doors and windows with no locks or broken locks, inadequate security lighting, garden tools left lying around and bushes that disguise access to windows, make thousands of homes easy targets for prospective burglars. Each year approximately 25 per cent of homes burgled throughout Australia are left unlocked, or have doors and windows left open. Empty drive-ways, uncollected junk mail, newspapers and inadequate lighting are easy give-aways to skilled thieves looking for empty homes during the holiday break.

Burglary is a major headache to insurance companies and for far too long, it would appear, the courts in many cases have seen fit to treat the offence with very light sentences.

It is debatable how much sentences can prevent further crime, but it is important that they reflect society's views.

In days of old theft at one time carried the death penalty or transportation to a far away penal colony. Society then changed its attitude a little and the death penalty for theft was abolished but replaced by very harsh and long gaol terms. Society again changed its attitude and as time progressed courts began to deal with burglars in a very lenient fashion.

In fact Society has changed its thinking to such a degree that the burglar in many cases can walk away scot free from a court after committing many burglaries, and insurance companies are left with huge payouts and, of course, the consumer is left to pay higher premiums to cover the cost of burglary.

Looking at how society has changed its way of thinking in relation to crime, one is reminded of the story of 'Little Red Riding Hood'. We all remember the 'old story': Little Red Riding Hood's mother asked her to take a basket of food to her sick granny who lived alone in the forest. On the same day a wolf was lurking nearby and decided to steal the goodies for himself.

The wolf hurried to granny's house, killed and ate the old lady and dressed himself in her nightie, then jumped into bed and waited for Little Red Riding Hood.

When she arrived at granny's house the wolf tried to grab her, resulting in the terrified child running screaming from the house. The woodcutter working nearby heard her screams, rushed to the house and killed the wolf with an axe saving Little Red Riding Hood.

The townspeople, learning of this great rescue proclaimed the woodcutter a hero and peace was restored to the forest.

But society's thinking must have changed, for at the inquest, the new version and certain 'facts' emerged. These were:

.   The wolf, before his execution had not been advised of his rights;

.   The woodcutter had given no warning before striking that fatal blow;

.   At the inquest, self-invited representatives of a civil liberties union stressed the point that although 'the act of killing and eating the old lady may have been in bad taste' actually the needy wolf was only hungry and merely 'doing his thing' and certainly did not deserve death;

.   Lawyers considered that killing granny could be construed as self-defence in as much as the wolf's basic intent was 'make love not war'. It could be reasonably assumed that granny resisted overtly and might, given the opportunity, have killed him! A psychiatrist testified that the wolf had not had an orthodox upbringing.

Based on these considerations, the judge decided that 'there was no valid legal basis for charges against the wolf' and that, in fact the woodcutter was guilty of assault with a deadly weapon. The woodcutter was sent for trial, later found guilty and sentenced to 99 years.

The night following the sentencing, the woodcutter's home was burnt to the ground. A year after the 'incident at granny's' her cottage was dedicated as a shrine to the wolf who had bled and died there.

Village officials spoke at the dedication, and Little Red Riding Hood gave a touching tribute. She explained that while she was grateful for the woodcutter's intervention, in retrospect she

realised that she had over-reacted. As she knelt and placed a
wreath in memory of the brave, martyred wolf everyone in the
forest wept.

Injustice isn't at all funny.

* * * * * *

THE ENGLISH SITUATION

Earlier in the seminar, the following questions about Neighbourhood Watch had been directed to Dr Paul Ekblom:

Q: How widespread is Neighbourhood Watch in England?

Ekblom: There are now over 42,000 separate Neighbourhood Watch
        schemes in England. They could be generally described as
        good neighbour schemes as they also involve general local
        surveillance, property marking and police circulars of
        local crime happenings.

Q: What formal training is provided for Neighbourhood Watch
        workers in England?

Ekblom: Individual police forces all have their own particular
        training courses. In addition, members of the public and
        local business people are involved in formal Crime
        Prevention Panels often chaired by local police.

Q: How is Neighbourhood Watch funded in England?

Ekblom: It is entirely voluntary.

Q: I believe Neighbourhood Watch schemes in England involve
        retired police officers who are paid a special
        allowance?

Ekblom: I am not sure of the extent of that practice, but it
        seems a good idea. As it is, in London where there are
        about 3,000 schemes, £6 million in police time is used
        to service them. In addition, some schemes use Voluntary
        Special Constables (to give advice) and long-term
        unemployed youths (to work on lock fitting programs or as
        hall porters in tower blocks of public housing).

* * * * * *

DISCUSSION

Q: I am concerned about your suggestion to concentrate
         on high-crime/low socio-economic areas. Couldn't that
         actually make crime worse there?

Wilson: That would seem unlikely - a Neighbourhood Watch scheme
         would hopefully encourage community spirit.

Q: Why do you emphasise citizen control of Neighbourhood
         Watch?

Wilson: I'm concerned about police using Neighbourhood Watch
         groups to advance their own ends, for instance to get
         more police.

Q: In Victoria, it was the State Executive of Neighbourhood
         Watch that decided to support the police campaign for
         more police. It was not engineered by the police. The
         police assist us, they do not instruct us or prop up
         Neighbourhood Watch groups for their own purposes.

Ekblom: It is always difficult to get an independent measure of
         displacement. The reported increase in car theft could
         have simply occurred anyway, despite the introduction of
         Neighbourhood Watch, couldn't it?

Mukherjee: Motor vehicle theft is very well reported and there
         was an overall increase in those offences. The
         comparison of those with burglaries shows that it really
         was displacement.

SELLING CRIME PREVENTION TO THE COMMUNITY

Jim King
Crime Prevention Section
Western Australian Police
Perth

From a police point of view, 'selling' crime prevention to the community is easy. As police officers working in the field of crime prevention, people listen to us. We have no vested interests. If we <u>were</u> actually selling some commodity, our task would be much more difficult.

Of course, what we are actually pushing is an idea, a concept. However, if 'selling' crime prevention is so easy for police Crime Prevention Officers (CPOs), why have we not achieved a reduction in crime? The answer is - there are not enough qualified CPOs doing the job. In Western Australia, there are nine CPOs, five of whom are fully committed to Neighbourhood Watch. The four remaining CPOs are continually engaged in traditional crime prevention activities. With a 'beat' of one million square miles and a population of 1.4 million people to serve, they are obviously very busy people.

Yet, on a population ratio, from my observations, the West is somewhat better off than most of the other states. The states with many more people have even less CPOs to deal with the problem.

WHICH DIRECTION TO GO

How can police administrators honestly expect such a small group to have any meaningful impact on reducing crime rates? In my view, we certainly have motivated many people in our community, however, we have continued to meet solid resistance from some within our own ranks. Police crime prevention has been in this country for twenty years. It has not developed, or been allowed to develop to its fullest potential. Why?

In my opinion, there are several answers to this question. Not the least of which is that many earlier police administrators did not understand or could see little value in what CPOs were trying to do. Unfortunately, the majority of operational police officers did, and still do, consider what CPOs are involved in, as not 'real police work' and often refer to us as 'plastic policemen'.

Crime prevention officers have missed many golden opportunities over the years. However, there is a light at the end of the tunnel, and for a change it is not a train coming the other way. This light is 'Community Policing'.

COMMUNITY POLICING - WHAT IS IT?

Community Policing, of course, is not new to those of us in crime prevention. It is an approach we have been pushing for many years. Our trouble has not been so much convincing the community, but, as already stated, convincing our own people of its worth.

This month, my Commissioner, Mr Bull, formerly adopted Community Policing as our Force's principal objective. The publication of a Community Policing Book for general distribution to the public indicates the importance the force places in the approach.

In my view, Community Policing means different things to different people and has yet to be clearly defined. I do not think it ever will be. It can mean a uniformed officer helping a little old lady across a busy street; it can be locking up a hardened professional criminal; being involved in Blue Light Discos; Neighbourhood Watch; joining a Service Club or teaching kids how to play football. The list is endless.

Why our police administrators are adopting this Community Policing concept so strongly is the real issue. In simple terms, police are not winning on the streets. Police budgets are being cut, and staff culled across the board. Detectives and other operational staff are chasing their tails on a continuous never-ending merry-go-round.

RECOGNISING PRIORITIES

Consideration of statistics of reported offences helps to explain the logic behind why many Police Departments are at last sitting up and taking notice of pro-active community policing programs.

In Western Australia in 1977, 57,000 offences were reported to the police. Ten years on, as at June 1987, 153,000 offences were reported. If you were running a business you would no doubt be very pleased at the 269 per cent increase. The fact is, we are running a business and spending large sums of public money doing it. Each year, approximately 55 per cent of all reported offences are listed as Stealing; 25 per cent as Breaking and Entering (commercial and domestic), and 10 per cent relate to Unauthorised Use of Motor Vehicles.

Added together, these represent 90 per cent of all reported offences. These figures are typical of all Australian jurisdictions. Why do people report these offences to the police? Generally speaking, it is a condition of their insurance. No report - no pay out! The question raised therefore is how much crime is not reported? I don't believe anyone really knows.

In my opinion, looking behind these figures will help understand where the true problem lies. Stealing, breaking and entering, and unauthorised use of motor vehicles are all offences where the victim and the offender do not confront each other. This of course poses a real problem as unwitnessed offences are difficult to solve and their clear up rates are 20 per cent or lower. Incidentally, of the 20 per cent cleared, over 50 per cent of the people responsible are aged between 7 and 17.

The remaining 10 per cent of the reported offences can be roughly divided in half, comprising fraud offences and what is often referred to as violent crime. Generally speaking, where the offender and the victim confront each other, arrest rates jump dramatically. For example, last year in Western Australia there was a 100 per cent clear up rate for murder and a rate of 80 per cent for serious assaults.

IDENTIFY THE PROBLEMS

A common denominator that links the offences of stealing, breaking and entering and the unauthorised use of motor vehicles together, is that with a little effort most could have been prevented. In particular, domestic burglaries, or home break-ins are a real headache in this country. To come to terms with the problem, it helps to think like thieves and identify their likes and dislikes.

There are obvious differences between homes and business premises. A thief wishing to attack a shop has most of the advantages in his favour. He can usually take as much time as he likes, make as much noise as he likes and use whatever equipment he likes.

In suburbia he shouldn't have it so easy.

Thieves do not like to be seen, heard, or made to waste precious time trying to gain entry. The trouble is, householders lay out the red carpet and for the opportunist thief it's Christmas Day every day in some of our residential streets. To add salt to the wound, 80 per cent of all offences against property in the suburbs take place during daylight hours.

TAKE UP THE CHALLENGE

We must seize this chance and do what we do best - educate and motivate. This particularly applies within police ranks.

In Western Australia we have started a program where new police officers are being instructed in basic crime prevention techniques. This will enable them to competently carry out home security appraisals. Before long, instead of having three or four CPOs tearing around the suburbs visiting very few homes, we will have 50 or a 100 - then more and more officers spreading our crime prevention ideas.

We must continue to strive to change operational police officers' attitudes to crime prevention. In the USA and other countries, operational police simply treat crime prevention (or community policing) as part of their everyday duties. The younger generation of overseas police cannot remember when it was not part of their day to day activities.

TAKE UP THE CHALLENGE

Unfortunately, in this country the vast majority of our community has the attitude, 'It won't happen to me', 'I'm covered by insurance', 'She's right mate'. You have heard it all before. The list is almost endless. This attitude is why our domestic break-in problem is totally out of proportion. It is much higher here than in most US cities. People in America lock their homes; they go out expecting to be broken into! This community awareness has done much to reduce that country's burglary problem. We must make people aware, make them share in the responsibility of protecting themselves and their property.

In my view, the hardest person to convince is the average Australian male. He takes our lifestyle for granted. For those of us who have travelled overseas, we see that the lifestyle we have in this country is not the norm, it is the exception.

Most men do not feel threatened on our streets or in their homes. Talking crime prevention to males can be an uphill battle. Nevertheless, it can be done, and in fact it must be done. How then? When talking on crime prevention to the community, there is a need to quickly identify the problem.

CRIME PREVENTION DEFINED

The definition of crime prevention is:

.   the anticipation, recognition and appraisal of a crime risk;

.   the initiation of some action to remove or reduce it.

This interpretation has been accepted by many countries throughout the world. However, when dealing with the public, there is a greater need to get to basics quickly rather than quote definitions.

Crime can be seen as involving a criminal, a victim, and the opportunity for a crime to be committed. There will always be victims. There will always be criminals. What we can vary dramatically is the opportunity.

Reducing opportunity for crime can be seen to involve three interlocking types of security - physical, electronic and procedural. Physical security includes such things as locks, solid doors and security screens. Electronic security includes such things as alarm systems, lighting, access control and CCTV. Procedural security involves people and behaviour and this is the weakest link. Where these three interlock is the safest place to be. It can be as simple as locking up your home, leaving a light and radio on and telling your neighbours you will be out.

SELLING HINTS

As a guide, when talking about security, there are four basic considerations: price, product, convenience, and installation.

Price is an important consideration. Very people will people say money is no object but CPOs must make their recommendations cost effective. In days gone by, after the CPO gave advice and left, the client started to get a few quotes and was frightened off by the price so usually ended up doing nothing!

By way of example, security screens fitted all round a house could cost $2,000. These days we suggest perhaps a security screen over a bedroom window and one somewhere else in the house to allow air to circulate with the other windows secured by a much cheaper method. Instead of paying $2,000 they pay $200.

Product knowledge is also vital. It is no good a CPO or police officer suggesting security equipment which will not work or failing to indicate its shortcomings. For example, when discussing with a home owner the installation of external security lighting which can be turned on from the main bedroom (or some other convenient spot), one should not fail to mention that a nocturnal intruder could simply lift the lid on the electricity box on the front verandah and pull out all the fuses!

The next important consideration is convenience. We are all creatures of habit; most of us are basically lazy and will usually take the line of least resistance. That is why many people these days are having home alarms installed. All they have to do on the way out is switch on their alarm. It beats running around the house, shutting and locking all the windows every time - people should still do this as well, but most do not.

Finally, if the average home handy person can install the recommended security device themselves, they are far more likely to purchase it.

CONCLUSION

In selling security, we do the best we can with the staff we have. In Western Australia we are very much aware of how people's attitudes towards security change after their property has been stolen. We now contact them as soon as possible after they report that they have been the victims of an offence.

We have all offence reports delivered to the Crime Prevention section every morning. A CPO selects any he or she thinks relevant and rings the complainant to offer crime prevention advice. We also try to have plenty of crime prevention literature available. It is important that the information is easy to obtain and understand. We also use the media whenever we can. They will usually assist. In addition most newspapers have a security supplement annually and they are always looking for editorial copy. The public are fickle, and need to be constantly reminded. Our friends within the media can do it best for us. In short, most CPOs will use whatever they can to punch their message out.

In Western Australia we hope, within five years, to have many operational police officers actively involved in crime prevention activities. By then we hope to have them accept it as a normal part of their duties and that in turn will help broadcast the importance of crime prevention throughout the community.

* * * * * *

DISCUSSION

Q: What is known about all those offenders between 7 and 17?

King: Not such a lot, but, in any event, 85 per cent of the kids seen by Juvenile Panels are never seen again.

Q: What do you think of legislation making parents responsible for their children's offending?

King: That could be a good idea, but what do you do if parents can't pay fines? Anyway, the biggest problem we face with 12 to 15 year olds is their being drunk on the streets.

Q: Isn't there a real problem that the people who most need security accessories are those who can least afford them?

King: To keep sane, we adopt a policy of helping those who try to help themselves. If they're really interested in equipment, there are some suppliers who will sometimes install gear for nothing.

Q: Is there evidence that property identification really works?

King: Well, certainly property can be easily returned to its owners but there's no solid Australian research.

Ekblom: The Home Office Crime Prevention Unit research found that the burglary rate did decrease after property identification.

Q: How can we Neighbourhood Watch workers assess and compare various security devices that are available?

King: Seek the impartial advice of a Crime Prevention Officer.

THE CRIME PREVENTION INDUSTRY

John Hopgood
Operational Planning Unit
Queensland Police
Brisbane

The Security Industry, like any organisation offering a service
to the community, has attracted considerable criticism about the
quality of its service, the need to provide the service and the
ability of personnel to undertake their tasks efficiently and
effectively. While the quality of security equipment (especially
electronic equipment) has developed to extremely high levels of
reliability, the industry still fails in the areas of personnel
and service.

SECURITY SYSTEMS AND FALSE ALARMS

An electronic security system in a major public facility will
incorporate the best equipment available and in the event of an
activation, is unlikely to affect the community. A security
system installed in a jeweller's premises, a warehouse, or even a
private home, may affect the community as that system does not
actually stop anyone committing anything - it just screams for
help. And what if nobody comes? The Queensland Police Force,
like all other Police Forces, is also affected by this
technology. In particular, the reliability of installations has
forced many Police Forces to take drastic decisions regarding
response to alarm signals.

In a recent survey undertaken by the Queensland Police Department, it was found that in the period 1986/87, 97.64 per cent of
alarm calls notified to the Police Operations Centre were found
to be 'false'. The estimated cost of attending those false
alarms was $250,753.39.

However, the number of calls attended to by Queensland police
officers had been halved since the previous survey in 1983/84.

This can be attributed to the greater use of monitored alarm
systems with private security monitoring stations arranging their
own patrols to attend, and a complacent community aware that
audible systems will automatically cut out within a pre-
determined time, and therefore not reporting active alarms to the
police.

This inherent false alarm factor has resulted in the South
Australia Police Force adopting a 'user pays' scheme of alarm
charging for police attendance. The scheme was introduced in

August 1984 and resulted in a dramatic decrease in false alarm calls in the first twelve months of operation, then a steady increase to a plateau equivalent to the situation prior to the introduction of the scheme.

New Zealand police went one step further and adopted a policy to respond only to those alarm activations found to be genuine. My interpretation of this policy is that they will investigate only after the commission of an offence. When it is realised that 32 per cent of police tasking in New Zealand related to alarm activations, considerable police man hours where being expended unnecessarily.

In Queensland, a new policy based on the South Australia Police experience has now been adopted and is at present being implemented in the Metropolitan Police Districts of Brisbane. It covers a 28 day period during which the first alarm is attended; the second alarm attracts a letter of warning and the third alarm is thoroughly investigated in order to make recommendations and requirements to be met prior to further attendance. A program of education in respect to alarm users has been implemented to encourage responsible attitudes amongst them. Further reviews could result in the introduction of a scheme by which people whose alarms malfunction must pay police for attendance.

The problems faced by police forces reflect on the Security Industry and the need for it to improve its quality of service. The level of technology has a great bearing on these matters, in that sales staff, installers, service staff and, in particular, patrol officers, are not totally aware of the complexities of modern security equipment.

LEGISLATION AND THE SECURITY INDUSTRY

The Security Industry is supposed to comprise professionals selling a professional service. Many times the final result is affected by the flavour of the month, for example, it may be a new generation of Passive Infra Detectors that, in the long run, may not provide the required protection. Naturally, the client also plays a part by playing one company against another, before making a final choice, and the challenge of the sale determines short cuts that can be achieved.

Western Australia Police took the initiative in 1976 with the introduction of the Security Agents Act. This legislation was described as being retrograde, but it did take positive steps to provide a means of regulating and ensuring a better quality of service within the industry in that State. When the Western Australian Parliament put security agents and guards under the licensing control of the police, fly-by-night companies and self-styled 'protection experts' - often with criminal records - disappeared within weeks. Another result of this legislation and the input of Crime Prevention Officers, was the development of the Australian Standards AS2803 and AS2804, covering the manufacture and installation of hinged security doors.

Improvements to the original Security Agents Act 1980 made Western Australia a leader in the field of the Security Industry, with the prime intention directed towards raising standards within the industry. Other jurisdictions have also acted with respect to private security personnel. New Zealand has enacted legislation; Canada, through its Law Reform Commission, prepared a study paper resulting in legislation; and the Victorian Parliament has received a 'Review of the Operations of the Private Agents Act of 1966'.

In 1983, Queensland Police commenced planning towards the introduction of a Commercial Security Agents Act. Research had shown increasing numbers of security personnel over the past few years. The only accountability under Queensland legislation for persons employed within the vast umbrella of the Security industry, is under the Invasion of Privacy Act 1971, which makes provision for the licensing of 'Private Inquiry Agents' and part of which allows them to act as guards or watchmen. The licensing under this Act ensures that people engaged as Patrol Officers can legally enter onto private property in the course of their employment. Despite current distractions, little has changed in this area.

The Queensland Police Department has not only drafted legislation guidelines, but during a series of briefings on the subject to all areas of the industry, outlined the perceived needs to be addressed in legislation in Queensland. It was considered that the industry in Queensland should be regulated to provide for the industry itself and the benefit of the public generally, a standard of conduct that would make it difficult for unsuitable people to penetrate the industry or for fraudulent operators or suppliers of sub-standard equipment to enter the market.

Where the industry was briefed and advised of the proposed legislation, adequate support was provided by the major employers of security personnel. The small operations, where employees are not generally licensed under the Invasion of Privacy Act as Sub Agents, lodged the greatest number of objections to the proposal. Claims of police control or that police were being employed by the major companies to assist in the demise of the smaller operator, were some of the more mentionable comments.

The end result was that the main objective of having the Security Industry assist in the development of standards applicable to all areas of the industry was wiped from the proposal. The resulting proposed legislation will do little to improve the quality of service, except in the extraction of licence fees.

During the development of the principal requirements for the legislation, the New South Wales Police requested a copy of the work that had been undertaken by Queensland. That led to the Security (Protection) Industry Act of 1985 being enacted in NSW. Many of the ideals that Queensland had aimed for are included in the NSW Act and, although there are areas where individuals will subsequently lodge complaints, the development of the Regulations will enable a greater degree of flexibility in the enhancement of standards.

UNDESIRABLE PRIVATE SECURITY PRACTICES

No doubt other States experience instances of people who are intent on achieving a 'quick killing' in the security market by, for instance, setting up business to sell inferior security products at greatly inflated prices. More often than not, the selling process is based on fear, and directed to people who are not in a position to afford quality security equipment, and must therefore use low weekly repayments of a hire purchase contract.

Generally within a short period of time, the equipment is unserviceable or the company providing the service no longer exists and the customer is faced with ongoing repayments for an item that is a burden.

One example of a high cost system is a particular radio transmitter-type intruder alarm system. For an outlay of $900, the purchaser receives a control unit, two transmitters and two open terminal magnetic reed switches. The equipment is marketed by a national organisation that works through a system of reselling. The company is not connected in any way with the Security Industry, but is able to market in Australia this install-it-yourself unit, imported as a package from the United States of America. The only part of the system that complies with the Australian Standard AS2201 is the back up battery. Such is the influence of this company, that the package was accepted as being a suitable alarm system for installation in a particular group of chemist shops in Queensland.

Crime Prevention Officers from all Australian police forces lodged letters of concern with the company, outlining the deficiencies in the system and recommending that the package be withdrawn from sale in Australia until a suitable system had been designed in compliance with the Australian Standards. The response by the company was to circulate their resellers with the advice that they were not professional security experts and could not advise on the installation of the systems, nor should they contact Crime Prevention Officers for any advice.

The point to be made is that after the initial purchase, which was two magnetic reed switches for $900 for the front and back door, all other accessories were optional and sold in multiples of $300. To adequately provide a suitable intruder alarm system based on this produce in a standard Australian home, would be an expensive proposition and even then the system could be disarmed at any point or at the main control panel, without activation. The company, despite further representation, is still engaged in promoting the original system.

A further undesirable practice is the door-to-door selling of security equipment, including window locks and simple magnetic reed switches for doors. Again the system of fear and hire purchase agreements is used to promote sales. One particular organisation has difficulty in recognising its own organisational name or telephone numbers and insists in aligning itself with reputable suppliers of intruder alarm equipment. When taken to task on the matter, the organisation sends letters of apology to the offended company and selects a further company to use as reference, in the knowledge that only about one in 20 people will actually make a telephone inquiry on the bona fides of the sales men or women.

While making inquiries into this company, the Queensland Police found that it expected to generate revenue of approximately $7 million for the current financial year. The majority of respectable and responsible companies would be happy with a similar result let alone a $2 company without any responsibilities.

There is another segment of the Security Industry that has been open to abuse and has attracted the fringe dwellers of respectability. An example is the 'expert' in the field of debugging, who makes a habit of finding transmitters in offices of high profile community leaders, naturally without a reliable witness present. He has also set up a security training school in Brisbane. For a modest fee of $800, which covers a 12 week course involving a total duration of 24 hours training, successful students receive another certificate to hang on the wall. Of course the relevant papers on how to be a security expert cost another $400, with a further option of paying a sizeable sum of money to establish yourself in business. This will entitle you to receive work from this person. If you wish to receive training in debugging methods, this course will cost another $1,800.

The Queensland Police have been unable to obtain further information on this particular aspect of training, as we have been unable to fulfil the financial requirements of the first course and are therefore not entitled to information on the more technical aspects of debugging.

As can be expected with this type of operation, the level of security training provided is extremely poor, with little real application to actual, responsible security industry situations.

Similar types of operations have previously been attempted in Queensland, but where there is little or not support from the Security Industry or Police, the credibility of the course proponents is quickly addressed.

There is a brighter side to aspects of training. The Queensland Confederation of Industry, together with the Commonwealth Employment Service (CES) and a firm known as PROSEC, have instituted a full ten week training course.

The normal considerations that CES apply to unemployed people must be met by people who attend the course, and currently there are fifteen attending. The subjects covered are ideal preparation for people employed by the Security Industry, covering matters such as the application of law, powers of arrest, site security, understanding alarm systems, aspects of patrolling and employer expectations, culminating in a five day outdoor self-development training exercise.

Although this is the first recognised attempt to organise and co-ordinate a concerted effort towards industry training in Queensland, the real test will be in the number of positions within the Security Industry that are offered to these potential employees. All of the recognised security companies in Brisbane have supported the scheme, however, there must arise a level of conflict between the training that has been undertaken by these people and the current expectations and practices of existing security companies.

Knowledge of available technology does not always transfer to practising security personnel such as patrol officers after an installation has been completed. The simple key is gradually being replaced by push buttons or electronic key pads, which enable a control panel to be programmed to handle a wide variety of functions.

It must be disconcerting for a patrol officer used to towing a heavy chain of keys over his shoulder for building checks, to suddenly be required to memorise or carry a register of key pad codes in addition to keys. There are some long standing and valued employees who commenced service with security companies in Brisbane as long ago as 1962 when they received three days of training. But since then they have had no further upgrading of training commensurate with the changes that have occurred.

Lack of knowledge by patrol officers extends to other areas, for instance, in how to use firearms and more importantly when to use a firearm. Patrol officers, like police, are continually being scrutinised on the application of the law, by a far more enlightened community. It is essential that front-line patrol officers within the Security Industry are continually updated on the legal barriers they will face and how best to encounter the difficult situations that arise.

These examples all relate to Queensland, but all Australian States would have similar situations. It is natural to draw on worst case scenarios or the most blatant of operations when drawing attention to shortcomings of an existing system. Where an intruder alarm system is properly installed, and sits quietly achieving its designed task, nothing is heard. When breakdowns occur and false alarms begin, all the world is to blame and from that time on, the alarm system attracts a reputation for unreliability. And seldom is reference made to the dedicated work of many patrol officers and the invaluable assistance they provide to Police Departments in detaining offenders or supporting police officers.

If the patrol officer is lucky, investigating police may recommend that some recognition be provided. This recognition could be by way of presentation of a plaque or a letter of thanks from the Department Head. Such recognition is essential for the morale of the patrol officer and for ensuring ongoing co-operation between the police, community and the Security Industry. These shortcomings create a sense of urgency for the development of suitable legislation for the Security Industry in Queensland.

CONCLUSION

With the continuing increase of crime and the adoption by Police Departments of Community Policing Programs, greater emphasis is now being placed on actual crime prevention. Education can only achieve a limited response from the community and then only those members of the community who have been affected by crime are likely to change their current security arrangements.

In order to achieve a marked improvement in security planning, the Security Industry must not only accept the changes in technology, but ensure that all employees adapt to the change in technology.

On the debit side, the following points are relevant in any consideration for the future:

1.   There are no enforceable standards or codes of conduct to guarantee performance of service.

    The current Australian Standards for alarm systems are adequate and applicable Australia wide, however, these are not generally recognised in law. Patrol services do not have, except where responsible companies designate policy, a general code of conduct for the actual method or manner in which the task should be undertaken.

2.   Anybody can set up in business as a 'Security Consultant', or other allied service area within the Security Industry, even though they may have a criminal record.

Even with legislation, there are still a number of grey areas. How do we deal with a person who established a business prior to the introduction of legislation and falls within the 'grandfather clause' of acceptance?

3. Will the development of enforceable standards improve the future of intruder alarm installations? The do-it-yourself expert, with his off-the-shelf components, will not be covered.

4. Security generally is an annoyance in our lives and to do the job properly it is expensive.

In the years ahead, considerations must be given to more than technical development. The industry must work towards achieving national standards which re capable of being enforced. To achieve this high aim, the image of recurring false alarms must certainly be corrected and an uncaring public shown that the Security Industry cares. Only then can we say we have not failed.

* * * * * *

DISCUSSION

Q: You complain about police attending false alarms - what would the police have been doing if they hadn't been doing that?

Hopgood:They could have been more visible in the country manning patrol cars.

Q: There are continuing problems with the NSW Security Protection Industries Act - there are difficulties with administration and there are no training courses to attend.

Hopgood:They are teething troubles. The legislation has the vision of a sort of apprenticeship in the security industry. That will help create a new generation of security professionals in the future.

Q: Isn't there a real conflict between crime prevention and certifying workers in the private security industry?

Hopgood:That typifies the resistance by the industry to change. A Crime Prevention Officer is familiar with the state of the art and with requirements in the industry. Regulation helps lead to greater awareness by everybody.

ANATOMY OF A CRIME PREVENTION PUBLICITY CAMPAIGN

Laurie Monaghan
Investigations Manager
NRMA Insurance Limited
Sydney

The NRMA is both a Motorist Association and an Insurance Company
that offers a range of services and domestic insurance products
to the community. Market penetration is extremely high communicating with 1.6 million members representing 39 per cent of the
adult New South Wales and Australian Capital Territory population
and indeed covering a broad spectrum of the New South Wales
community. Therefore, the NRMA's capacity to communicate to a
wide audience is particularly strong, although the effectiveness
of any communication is very much dependent on a range of other
factors.

For some years, the NRMA has been a most active participant in
community awareness programs, including several crime prevention
campaigns. Its most recent crime prevention campaign against car
theft was launched in May, 1987, and it is this particular
campaign that will be discussed in this paper.

Mass media campaigns, although relatively new, are increasingly
being used as a crime control strategy. Many of these campaigns
have been designed to encourage victims to take simple
precautions to reduce opportunities, but various research studies
strongly suggest that crime prevention advertising has, in
itself, failed to produce changes in the behaviour of potential
victims towards improving their security behaviour (Riley and
Mayhew, 1980). It has also been suggested that such a
concentrated crime message might also result in unintended and
unwanted effects, for instance, by stimulating the extent of
public agreement with undesirable reactions to crime. There is
indeed a persuasive range of arguments opposing the use of crime
prevention awareness campaigns.

In the light of this knowledge, why did the NRMA embark upon a
car theft awareness campaign, given also the extraordinary costs
associated with mounting such a campaign? Riley and Mayhew
somewhat cynically suggest in their study that '... publicity is
both easy to do and likely to protect (the campaigner) from a
charge of complacency about crime' (1980:13, my emphasis). This
was not the NRMA view of the recent campaign 'Make Life Hell for
Car Thieves', although I cannot be certain about the intentions
of the previous NRMA campaigns in 1983 and 1985, as I was not a
participant in their preparation.

What then was the 'Make Life Hell for Car Thieves' campaign
about, and what set it apart from previous campaigns in terms of
approach and ultimately, effectiveness?

Firstly, I think it is important to understand the effectiveness
of this strategy as it relates specifically to the problem of car
theft. Car theft, like any other criminal or social problem, is
a very complex phenomenon. It has unique qualities that set it
apart from other crimes and, consequently, it requires a variety
of preventive strategies. It certainly will not be susceptible
to solution through any single prevention initiative. Thus, the
campaign's crime prevention capabilities are seemingly restricted
by the multi-faceted nature of car theft.

In order to appreciate the thrust of the campaign, it is useful
to know what type of people operate as car thieves and, in turn,
what are the appropriate measures needed to reduce their criminal
activity. This can best be achieved in the form of a matrix of
actions and reactions. This is derived from analysis and
conjecture applied to the situation in NSW. In itself it does
not assume complete precision, but offers our best intellectual
estimates of the situation. It is perhaps indicative of the car
theft problem that we cannot be certain that the problem in other
States resembles that in NSW. Such is the lack of objective and
factual information pertaining to the other States.

The largest proportion of car thefts are attributed to joy-riders
and account for approximately 55 per cent of offences reported to
the police. These joy-riders may or may not damage the vehicle
in some way. The damage may be vandalism, theft of some items
or crash damage. The NRMA estimates that this type of offender
accounts for $30 million of the total cost associated with car
theft. In the crime prevention context, it is this type of
offender who might be deterred by increased public awareness,
which is one target of the NRMA campaign.

In the past, NRMA campaigns have been centred on 'lock-your-car'
publicity. Their value in reducing theft has not been
sufficiently evaluated to comment on their success or otherwise.
However, overseas evidence from more detailed evaluations
indicate that such campaigns provide little success in improving
security behaviour (Riley and Mayhew, 1980; Burrrows et al,
1979). In these two campaigns, those authors describe the levels
of reported thefts, and of the proportion of cars found secure in
spot checks by the police, revealed no demonstrable effect from
either campaign in terms of these measures.

It is suggested by Clarke (1987) that one possible reason for the
failure of these campaigns is that the existing community
practice may already be close to the optimum level of voluntary
compliance possible. In other words, it would require some form

of intervention, such as the introduction of central or automatic car locking systems, legislation and the like, to raise the level of security compliance further. The reasons for this are several, but the principal view is car owners perceive a low probability of victimisation. The 'it can't happen to me' mentality is all too pervasive, making it hard to change ingrained habits. In brief, car owners' security habits appear to reflect subjective perceptions of the overall risk of car theft and the risk faced in particular situations (Research Bureau Limited 1977).

In the current NRMA campaign, certain other planned benefits were considered and subsequently occurred. One such planned benefit was the increased corporate identification that would result from campaign penetration. It would be naive to suggest the NRMA was not concerned with the potential corporate relations gain in mounting the campaign. A significant boost to the timing of the campaign launch was that the problem of car theft was beginning to attract both Government and community attention. In turn, the campaign was able to generate concern about car theft and significantly raise its profile as a crime problem. This has resulted in a considerable range of initiatives being considered and/or implemented by the Government over the last few months.

I think it is also fair to say the NRMA were aware the campaign would be limited in producing any behavioural changes of potential victims, unless, they focused the campaign on other areas apart from simply persuading drivers to lock their vehicles. The important distinction which has set it apart from previous campaigns, and for that matter similar overseas campaigns, is that it was able to disseminate a great deal of detailed information to the community concerning the particular risks they run, depending on where they live, where they park their cars and what types of vehicles they drive.

An interesting footnote to this risk identification process is that the NRMA launched the campaign – intended particularly for television coverage – at Sydney's worst location for stolen vehicles, the Westfield Shopping Complex at Parramatta. To Westfield management's credit they agreed to the launch and have since improved security at the complex, resulting in a decline in the car theft rate of 40 per cent compared to the same period in 1986.

Following the launch, the campaign went into a 'burst' mode of publicity, supported by appropriate media releases and a research document, entitled, Car Theft in New South Wales (NRMA, 1987). The initial launch was bolstered the next day by a seminar, entitled, 'Car Theft: Putting on the Brakes', jointly organised by the Australian Institute of Criminology and the NRMA.

The campaign maintained intensity for several weeks through the various media forums and the NRMA distribution network in the following way:

. All NRMA branches had information packs, containing five separate brochures, available for distribution. 100,000 were given out on request in the first eight weeks and 50,000 more have been printed.

. All metropolitan branches displayed a large banner showing the theme of the project and had combi-vision (electronic poster system) presentations of photographs and message. The major branches screened a continuous video display.

. A community service television message was screened on the three Sydney commercial channels in both paid and community service slots. Regional and country channels were offered the announcement to screen as community service.

. A half-page newspaper advertisement and associated editorial was the basis of a supplement in all Cumberland newspapers, reaching an estimated readership of 1.5 million. Other NSW newspapers used the NRMA editorial to run special features.

. Shopping centre displays were mounted in the 12 most affected suburbs, using a continuous video. Brochures were distributed.

. Theatre ads were run for up to 13 weeks in selected Village and Hoyts Theatres to reach young people.

. Reinforcement of the campaign came from editorials and feature stories in the NRMA's official journal, 'The Open Road' (readership 1.5 million).

. 1.48 million NRMA envelopes (3-4 months usage) were overprinted with the campaign theme. The theme was also used as a tagline on the 'Dial-it' NRMA Road Service Report.

The NRMA's ultimate aim was to maintain a controlled level of continuity of message rather than an intensive one. Its fear was that it might ultimately confront a problem of diminishing returns with a too intensive coverage resulting in boredom and over-exposure. It was felt the awareness process would work best when the major publicity operated in 'bursts' with an underlying communication approach providing the continuity and important reinforcement effect. This latter approach was achieved through Neighbourhood Watch schemes, which the NRMA sponsors in the Australian Capital Territory and co-sponsors in NSW.

The Neighbourhood Watch program has two attractive features for those running crime prevention campaigns. Firstly, it involves people who are acutely aware of crime, are participating in crime prevention initiatives, and are therefore more susceptible to changing security behaviour. Secondly, Neighbourhood Watch groups provide much needed impetus and renewed community interest in the program, through that all very important communication called feedback. Researchers have documented the decline in participation and discontinuation of Watch programs that frequently occurs with the passage of time. One of the main problems is the single issue focus of many Watch groups (Rosenbaum, 1987) and car theft awareness at least has provided another community issue on which to engender interest.

It is evident from NRMA meetings with Neighbourhood Watch groups that car theft awareness is high and the groups are anxious to obtain more information about the problem in their area and learn what prevention ideas they can use in their daily routine. However, Neighbourhood Watch is not a complex strategy for shaping social behaviour but rather a simple program designed to encourage people to take individual prevention measures to avoid victimisation, watch for suspicious behaviour and call the police if necessary.

RESEARCH

As indicated earlier, the thrust of the campaign centred on the NRMA research document, Car Theft in New South Wales. The campaign research itself fell into three broad areas:

- Test the likely effectiveness of the communication programs, ie the logo, slogan and TV community service announcement, with its target audience prior to the campaign launch.

- Establish a benchmark measure of people's attitudes to car theft.

- Measure the changes in attitudes following the communication campaign. This was supplemented by a vehicle security survey conducted before and after the campaign.

The research was conducted in three phases:

- A qualitative investigation of the effectiveness of the communication media planned for the campaign.

- A quantitative benchmark survey administered prior to the commencement of the campaign.

- A quantitative tracking survey administered within a fortnight of the completion of the campaign.

The methodology is explained in more detail in the Final Report from PA Consulting Group (1987) who conducted the field research on behalf of NRMA. The sampling process produced a random sample of 1,223 people seen as a reliable group with which to track the effectiveness of the campaign. A further tracking survey of 600 motor vehicle owners was drawn at random from telephone subscribers in metropolitan Sydney, Newcastle and Wollongong. They responded to a questionnaire which covered the same issues as the benchmark questionnaire and also addressed the recall of three elements of the public awareness campaign, namely the TV advertisement, the 'Make Life Hell for Car Thieves' kit and articles in 'The Open Road' magazine.

At this early stage, the NRMA believes the community is aware of the size of the car theft problem but not the true dollar cost of car theft. However, the threat of car theft is not perceived as enough of a personal threat to motivate individuals to greatly change their behaviour. The active use of devices to deter theft is low. This behaviour appears to arise from three sources:

- A belief that no deterrent device is capable of stopping the determined, professional thief.

- Greater importance being given to convenience rather than theft deterrence when using a motor vehicle.

- The commodity status of the motor vehicle among the male and youth population.

One interesting feature is that the community firmly believes the responsibility for reducing car theft lies directly with the individual motor vehicle owner - once the Government and manufacturers provide the proper support. Moreover, programs aimed at public awareness or at developing community vigilance are regarded as likely to be effective in contributing to reducing theft by prompting people to use individual actions such as:

- Locking doors and windows;

- Ensuring valuables are not visible in the vehicle;

- Taking care in parking.

The element of the campaign which deals with deterrent action can be considered the most valuable part of the campaign. The image attached to the NRMA name reinforces the perceived community service nature of the campaign.

While the campaign is perceived as being valuable and in keeping with the NRMA image, there is no indication of any immediate attitude change in the time since the completion of the campaign. However, a trend did appear with the perceived effectiveness of individual care solutions and high community-based solutions such as Neighbourhood Watch ranking more highly in the tracking survey.

From further research it was found that 20 per cent of car alarms and ignition fuel cut-off switches fitted to vehicles from the sample were fitted in the last three months which tends to connect the campaign with this recent trend. Interestingly, 79 per cent of the sample believe that offering a discount on insurance would be effective in encouraging people to fit anti-theft devices. However, when choosing an insurance company, discounts of this sort were considered not very important in the decision to insure with a particular company.

It is clearly too early to determine the effectiveness of the campaign with regard to behavioural changes. Preliminary sample analysis of police car theft reports indicates a general decline in the theft rate compared to the same period in 1986. However, further analysis taking into account both time and specific comparisons of car and other crime statistics is necessary before attributing any real effects of the campaign to the declining trend.

On another front, car security surveys conducted by the NRMA during 1987 show an improvement in drivers' security behaviour following the campaign's peak, but again the information is only preliminary and more work needs to be done in this area.

More positively, the campaign produced approximately 350 news-paper articles mentioning the campaign or using NRMA comment on car theft. A further 70 known newspaper articles have been printed relating to car theft and are believed to have been generated by the campaign. All the TV channels covered the launch of the campaign and followed up with feature programs on car theft including the '60 Minutes' program.

One interesting criminological development saw a District Court Judge impose heavy gaol sentences on convicted car thieves after having read in open court excerpts from the editorial in the NRMA magazine 'The Open Road', referring to car theft as having reached plague proportions.

I will simply conclude with the remarks from the British researchers, Heal and Laycock on crime prevention publicity. They write, 'promotional activity must create a climate within which prevention is seen to be the sensible and intelligent thing to do' (1986:132). I believe the NRMA campaign has achieved that aim with the community and prompted the government to take action on car theft. The results so far are encouraging but only time will provide the real test of the campaign's success.

REFERENCES

Burrows, J.P., Ekblom, P. & Heal, K. (1979), Crime Prevention and the Police, Home Office Research Study No. 55, HMSO London.

Clarke, R.V.G. (1987), 'Crime Prevention - Car Theft Strategies', in Car Theft - Putting on the Brakes, pp 6-12, NRMA, Sydney.

Heal, K. and Laycock, G. (1986), Situational Crime Prevention - From Theory Into Practice, HMSO, London.

Liddy, D. (1987), Car Theft - A Strategy Needed, Paper presented at the Australian Automobile Association Symposium on Car Theft, Canberra, November 1987.

Monaghan, L. (1987), 'Community Awareness and Prevention of Car Theft', in Car Theft - Putting on the Brakes, pp 33-37, NRMA, Sydney.

NRMA (1987), Car Theft in NSW, NRMA, Sydney.

PA Consulting Group (1987), Effectiveness of Anti-Theft Public Awareness Campaign Conducted by the NRMA, Mimeo, Sydney.

Research Bureau Ltd (1977), Car Theft Campaign Evaluation 1976-1977, Prepared for Central Office Information, London.

Riley, D. & Mayhew, P. (1980), Crime Prevention Publicity: An Assessment, Home Office Research Study 63, HMSO, London.

Rosenbaum, D. (1987), 'The Theory and Research Behind Neighbourhood Watch: Is It A Sound Fear and Crime Reduction Strategy?', Crime And Delinquency, 33, pp 103-134.

* * * * * *

DISCUSSION

Q: Neighbourhood Watch is stopping a lot of property crime, and therefore stopping many insurance claims but nothing is coming back to the community from the insurance companies.

A: Insurance companies support Neighbourhood Watch around Australia at considerable cost. They have actually been most generous to the Watch programs themselves and to police forces supporting them.

93

Q: Nevertheless, there are some Watch groups who have great
        trouble funding their activities.   Couldn't special
        grants be made to help them?

A: The sponsors provide funds for the whole program, not for
        individual groups, that would be quite unmanageable.

Q: Perhaps the wealthier groups could help out their poorer
        colleagues?

Coster: Yes, there are certainly differences.   One Victorian
        Watch group has assets of over $20,000.

CRIME PREVENTION IN THE WORKPLACE:

CRIME IS A SYMPTOM, BAD MANAGEMENT THE DISEASE

Ray Brown
Loss Prevention Consultant
Business Abuse Prevention System Pty Ltd
Jolimont, Victoria

My experience over the last ten years in Loss Prevention
management in private enterprise has convinced me that a
positive, pro active, employee involved program is the most cost-
effective, and potentially the most productive, approach that can
be taken to reduce deviance in the workplace. Business must
involve its best resources - its people - in reducing illegal,
unethical and irresponsible activities in the workplace. The
benefits of a successful program will be measured in nett profit,
healthier work environment and positive attitude towards loss
prevention.

The public's perception of crime is generally based on the local
'Crime Rate' which in turn is usually based on crimes reported to
the police. In the business community, however, there is no
readily acceptable measure of crime. The lack of standardised
definitions and classifications, and the under-reporting of
workplace crime, contribute greatly to problems of measurement.

THE EXTENT OF WORKPLACE CRIME

In the United States, ten per cent of the Gross National Product
is estimated as the disappearance rate in the business sector.
That equates to US$40 billion. Applied to Australia the loss to
business through workplace deviance is around $2.5 billion each
year.

The Retail Industry in Australia estimates its losses through
theft and deviance as two per cent of sales. That is
conservative and relates more to the large retailers who have
good stock controls and ability to assess product loss. The
annual loss - $800 million.

The Australian Federal Police has submitted a report to the
Government which alleges an annual $4 billion worth of offences
against Federal Departments. The real cost may be up to
$9 billion which would wipe out Australia's national debt.
(Those figures, incidentally, do not take into account the cost
of fraud offences against the six State Governments). Average
business people do not know what they are losing through employee
deviance. If they think it is not happening to them, then they

are wrong. In the past three months I have talked to numerous retailers of all types and sizes and to a large variety of other businesses including oil companies, banks, State Government utilities, manufacturers and distributors. There has not been one who does not have a problem.

It may not be clear cut criminal behaviour, but every business has examples of unethical, irresponsible or illegal behaviour which cause loss of profit, productivity and morale.

In 1985 at the National Retail Crime Prevention Council (NRCPC) conference, Stephen Mugford of the ANU and Bill Cherrey from Phillip Institute in Melbourne, both eminent and outspoken academics made it clear that 'fiddling', 'deviant workplace behaviour', and 'theft', are part of human nature, and need to be addressed in that light (Challinger, 1986).

In my opinion, the work of Clark and Hollinger (1981) is the most comprehensive, objective research into the extent and cause of employee theft and counterproductive behaviour in the work setting. The Clark-Hollinger philosophy has become for me the clear guide for tackling workplace losses of all types.

The study was conducted in two phases over a three year period. Forty seven business corporations in three major cities (Minneapolis/St. Paul, Cleveland and Dallas/Forth Worth) were surveyed. These comprised 16 retail department store chains, 21 general hospitals, and 10 electronic manufacturing firms. The total number of people employed in each company at the time varied from as few as 150 in the smaller firms to over 10,000 in the large multi-location companies.

Data was acquired by two methods. First, in a random sampling of all occupational levels, 9,175 employees anonymously returned completed questionnaires. Second, 247 personal interviews were conducted with key management executives, including, when possible, the Chief Executive Officer, personnel manager, operations manager, and security director. In addition, face-to-face interviews were conducted with 256 employees from six of the participating companies in Minneapolis/St. Paul.

Clark and Hollinger make it very clear that one of the most important findings from their study is that the majority of people are not stealing. They found that the level of deviance or theft in an organisation had very little to do with the size or sophistication of the security apparatus or security operations internally. However, the organisations that had lower levels of deviance had some common traits. Those organisations had very clearly defined and well communicated company policy. Their budget for security, or the number of security personnel did not seem to have an impact, although they were companies where the employees perceived that the company was security conscious.

Common excuses such as, 'we've got a factory or a store on the bad side of town, that's why we have employee thefts', had no correlation with deviance. Clark and Hollinger found no relationship to factors outside the workplace.

The organisations with lower deviance were a product of a number of factors that Clark and Hollinger call 'humane' and which applied to that particular workplace. Thus, even within the same company one location could have a higher level of deviance than the next. They may have had the same corporate policies, but there were other factors that affected deviance.

What they found was that if there is a work environment or workplace where employees are dissatisfied, and feel that management is taking advantage of them, higher deviance is likely.

Related to deviance in particular locations are factors such as evidence of management conflict, general treatment of employees, and management's enforcement of rules. Simply having the rules set down is one thing. It's not just the written policy, it's how they are communicated at the particular location, how they are enforced there, how the people are treated there, and what the values of the group are there. Deviance is not a product of what is happening in a community; a company in each location creates its own environment.

PROPERTY THEFT

Property theft is not the only form of employee deviance. There is a strong relationship between taking of property and other behaviours which Clark and Hollinger call production deviance. They include drug abuse, the abuse of sick leave, and in the retail sector, the abusing of the staff discount privilege.

From the viewpoint of employers and management, there is persuasive evidence that the factors associated with property theft also prompt production deviance. These include sloppy workmanship, sick leave abuse and other counterproductive activities. The theft of company property is also a deviant act against the interest of the organisation.

If you are interested in reducing employee theft and deviance, you must have a sensitivity to the perceptions of employees in the workforce. Dissatisfied employees admitted being more frequently involved in property and production deviance.

In particular, younger workers may have a feeling of alienation and believe that older people are getting all the benefits. Consequently, they may be more likely to try and get their own benefits through other means. But one simply can't nail everything down. Security hardware such as cameras, one way glass, mirrors and so on may be a deterrent to outside thieves, but when directed at employees it tends to convey a message of distrust. Research suggests that social controls, not physical controls, are in the long run the best deterrence to theft and deviance within the organisation. (Although there is still room for hardware in the traditional sense).

A clear policy relating to theft must be formulated by management. That policy must be continually disseminated through the workforce. The typical fifteen minute overview during new employee orientation is not adequate. Presentations about ethical standards are frequently overwhelmed, in the pre-employment orientation program, by more immediate task information. Education and training programs must continually restate that taking company property is theft, and will be sanctioned.

The structure of company operating standards must also reflect anti-theft policy and double standards should be avoided. At the moment, a Senior Manager of a company who embezzles $60,000, but has contacts with key clients, may be dealt with differently from a cashier who steals $6,000. The cashier will be prosecuted. That's unfortunately the way that kind of system works.

The use of threat probably does more harm than saying nothing about the subject. Privately sanctioning specific acts does nothing to deter others, whether presently stealing or considering involvement. To obtain general deterrence, these specific sanctions should not occur in a vacuum. Announcing to the workforce that a number of employees have been sanctioned for theft may allow the remaining employees to realistically calculate the risk of their getting caught for deviance.

Employees often do not even know whether the person was prosecuted, or whether the person had to pay back. They need to know if the thief was caught, that the employer took swift action, and simply will not allow theft to occur without sanction.

In general, I have found that applying a law enforcement mode to internal theft does not work very well. The most effective role of security staff in deterring theft by employees is in communicating the roles that other departments such as inventory control, finance and personnel play in implementing the company policy on theft activity. The experience of security personnel with cases of theft frequently highlights the critical role played by supervisors or co-workers.

Firms with the least theft are characterised by a consistent message from all departments within the organisation, not just security, that theft is not acceptable behaviour. The companies

experiencing the most theft, are those who signal to employees
that they are neither concerned about their property or their
employees.

Based on employee interviews, it would appear that the exact
definition of property and production deviance is continually
being constructed in the workplace. The workplace and the people
who work there will determine what is acceptable - what's theft
and what's not theft.

If everybody takes one item, that's not theft. But, is two items
theft? If someone is arrested for two items, that becomes theft.
But until we find that level, it's going to be determined by the
norms of the group. If it's not clearly communicated, employees
will effectively define it.

You will only be productive in security and loss prevention if
your employees take some part of the responsibility. There is no
expert, no manager, no security person, no company owner, no
camera or anything that could be as effective as preventing theft
and deviance as an individual person. It doesn't matter what
their educational level or their expertise. They don't have to
be an interviewer or an investigator - the single best loss
prevention resource is the average person because that average
person will either contribute to theft, or they won't. It's that
simple. It's a matter of whether or not people do the right
thing. The challenge becomes how to get people to do that.

A lot of business abuse is not dishonesty: it's incompetence;
it's indifference, it's ignorance. All of these activities are
unethical and international. Instead of the term deviance - I
prefer to use the phrase business abuse. That can be defined as
any illegal, unethical or irresponsible act that causes loss or
harm to a company.

REDUCING BUSINESS ABUSE

People are the world's best loss prevention resource. Every
person has the potential so what's the problem? Business abuse
is a people related issue; an issue that can only be successfully
addressed through education and management. Why do we exist?
Why does the company need us?

Traditionally in security, most of the money has been spent on
the three per cent of people who are deviant. We should spend
a little bit of the money on the other 97 per cent and spend
a little bit of time on these people. By ignoring the good
people you are allowing them to become corrupted and forcing them
at the workplace to become the bad guys. Let's separate the good
guys from the bad guys.

Why don't these good people currently contribute? They don't
contribute because because they're ignorant; they don't know what

causes shortage, they have not been told. They may not even know what the rules are. How can anybody contribute in circumstances when they have no understanding?

The second difficulty is that while people probably know they should say something, there is a barrier; they don't feel comfortable, or they think it's not their job. They may feel they will be subject to harm or harassment if they come forward. The third difficulty is a matter of perception. That includes feelings like 'this company makes a ton of money. I'm not getting paid enough, and everyone does it. What's a packet of biscuits? What's five dollars? I handle ten thousand dollars a day.'

The focus in a prevention program must be on trying to beat these barriers and that's our objective, to slowly but surely shift those barriers and it has to go on forever. It is worthwhile and important to identify to the majority of good employees some of the intangible costs to them of having business abuse occur at their workplace. Having to be bag searched, having to be observed by cameras. That's a cost to them as honest people. Why do they have to suffer that? The company should explain the reason is that people have taken things and that such security practices could be relaxed a little if all employees worked towards preventing their fellow employees from engaging in business abuse.

REFERENCES

Challinger, D. (1986), Retailers and Crime Today, National Retail Crime Prevention Council, Canberra.

Clark, J.P. and Hollinger, R.C. (1983), Theft by Employees, Lexington Books, Lexington.

CRIME PREVENTION IN THE WORKPLACE:

A RETAIL PERSPECTIVE

John Rice
Chairman, National Retail Crime Prevention Council
and National Loss Prevention Manager
Target (Australia) Pty Ltd
Geelong, Victoria

There are ten key initiatives to be considered when addressing the control of employee dishonesty. These initiatives are not specific to the retail environment, the basic principles are common to all areas of commerce and industry.

1. DEVELOP AND PROMULGATE AN UNDERSTANDABLE AND UNAMBIGUOUS POLICY STATEMENT THAT CLEARLY DEFINES WHAT IS CONSIDERED DEVIANT BEHAVIOUR, FOR WHICH DISCIPLINARY ACTION WILL BE TAKEN.

In all workplaces there are perks, privileges and fiddles going on, many involving minor acts of dishonesty. Generally these activities are tolerated by management and supervisors who, in fact, may set the limits and allow employee participation to achieve productivity objectives.

In many workplaces these perks and privileges have been built into employees' working and reward conditions and are seen as a form of job enrichment and compensation for poor working conditions.

However, it is critical when dealing with employee deviance that there is a clear understanding and acceptance of what is to be tolerated as a perk, and what will be considered deviant behaviour, so there can be no misunderstanding or dispute when an employee is to be sanctioned for a breach of policy.

Without this clear definition of right and wrong, all other initiatives to prevent employee theft must fail.

2. ESTABLISH A CLEARLY DEFINED LEGAL, MORAL AND FAIR SANCTION POLICY FOR DEALING WITH DETECTED DEVIANT EMPLOYEES.

Employees must know and expect what will happen to them if they commit a breach of the deviant behaviour policy, there can be no argument that they did not understand the consequence of their action.

There are a number of important points to consider when putting together a sanction policy. Merely resorting to the criminal justice system may satisfy the desire to see the offender punished, but it may not be in the best interests of the company, especially where the offence is of a minor nature and the offender is a highly trained, productive employee.

Dismissal and prosecution may not be cost effective, they may lead to serious employee relations problems, and may attract bad publicity, all to the detriment of the organisation.

It would seem that a more tolerant view is taken of first offender shoplifters, who may merely receive a warning, whereas employees with previously unblemished records may be both dismissed from employment and prosecuted in court. The punishment should not only be commensurate with the offence, but should also suit the overall needs of the individual and the organisation.

No matter what approach is taken to develop a sanction policy, the consequences must be applicable to employees at all levels of the organisation, there can be no two tier system to differentiate between management and staff.

3. HAVE A STRUCTURED PRE-EMPLOYMENT SCREENING PROCEDURE TO CATER FOR ADEQUATE CHECKING OF PROSPECTIVE EMPLOYEES AT ALL LEVELS OF THE ORGANISATION.

Obviously, it is critical to ensure, as far as is practicable, that persons to be employed are honest, stable and reliable; such a procedure not only eliminates high risk applicants, it can also strengthen the attitudes of honesty in staff who are hired.

It is no longer sufficient to ask a person to fill out an application for employment, conduct cursory checks with one, perhaps two previous employers, and then accept that person to a position of trust within the organisation.

There are a number of elementary initiatives that should be undertaken to eliminate high risk applicants. The first important step is to obtain the applicant's written consent to make all necessary enquiries to verify the details of the application.

The key areas of verification are: proof of identity, age, qualifications, and previous employment, criminal history checks, financial standing checks, and compensation claim checks.

Widely used and accepted in America, but rarely used in Australia are the so called paper and pencil psychological tests that claim to identify high risk applicants in the areas of honesty, violent emotional instability and drug abuse.

Drug and alcohol abuse in the workplace, with a corresponding increase in property and production deviance is an escalating problem in the USA and this is evidenced by the emergence there of urine analysis as a pre-employment screening initiative to identify drug users.

4. <u>IMPLEMENT AND MAINTAIN A DETAILED INDUCTION PROGRAM FOR ALL NEW EMPLOYEES THAT PROVIDES FOR THEIR UNDERSTANDING AND ACCEPTANCE OF THE DEVIANCE AND SANCTION POLICY AND PROVIDES BROAD EXPOSURE TO KEY LOSS PREVENTION REQUIREMENTS.</u>

Pre-employment screening hopefully provides honest employees for the workplace, and a detailed induction program is the first essential step in maintaining that honesty. New employees should be given into the care of a sponsor, a senior experienced employee, who is responsible for ensuring that the induction process is properly completed.

As each state of the induction is completed, the understanding and acceptance of the policy and procedure points covered should be acknowledged by the employee, and verified by the sponsor, by both signing an appropriate document which should be filed with the employee's staff history card. This negates the opportunity for employees to disclaim lack of knowledge or understanding on matters in dispute at a later stage.

There have been studies that suggest that dishonesty in many cases starts after the employee starts work, and that the majority of internal theft is committed by workers who were honest when they were hired. If this is so, a non-existent or deficient induction process for new employees would seem the most probable cause.

5. <u>DEVELOP DETAILED TRAINING PROGRAMS TO PROGRESSIVELY EXPOSE EMPLOYEES TO ALL LOSS PREVENTION POLICY, PROCEDURE AND REGULATIONS: SUPPORT THIS TRAINING WITH ONGOING AWARENESS PROGRAMS THAT BOTH RE-ITERATE THE LOSS PREVENTION CONCEPT, AND MAINTAIN EMPLOYEE COMMITMENT TO THAT CONCEPT.</u>

It is pointless to have detailed policy and procedure on loss prevention matters unless the objectives and requirements are fully understood, accepted and followed by staff. Understanding and acceptance can only be obtained if employees are informed of not only what has to be done, but why it has to be done.

Loss prevention training needs for all levels of management and staff must be identified and appropriate packages developed to meet these needs. Programs and schedules must then be developed and implemented to ensure all staff are adequately trained within a reasonable time frame.

Concurrent with formalised training needs, staff awareness programs must also be developed and run so that the loss prevention message is constantly brought to the attention of all employees, and their attitude and commitment constantly reinforced. Awareness programs can take a number of forms, usually centred on a common title or catch phrase. Posters, bulletins, information boards, pay envelope stuffers and competitions are all useful methods of maintaining staff awareness.

6. HAVE A SIMPLE BUT EFFECTIVE SYSTEM OF ASSET INVENTORY CONTROL THAT READILY IDENTIFIES LOSSES AND PRECIPITATES INVESTIGATIVE ACTION.

Obviously, if employees are aware that the theft of an item of merchandise, or an amount of cash will be detected and investigated, the probability of their offending is significantly diminished.

The most basic inventory control is a regular stocktake procedure that identifies unknown losses by comparison of the book stock value of merchandise against the actual value of the stock on hand. Mini-stock counts can be conducted on known high theft risk lines, discrepancies readily identified, and corrective action taken. Recording of all identified known theft is also useful, that is, every empty packet or discarded swing ticket can be collected on a daily basis and collated to establish theft patterns. Sophisticated point of sale control systems can readily identify anomalies and provide exception reports on register operators with poor performance patterns.

All of these controls, and the results obtained, must be disseminated to employees who must be made aware of the high probability of theft identification and detection. Most importantly, identified theft must be vigorously investigated to show employees that there is a high level of concern, and that theft will not be tolerated.

7. DEVELOP AND IMPLEMENT PROCEDURAL CONTROLS THAT MAKE THEFT MORE DIFFICULT AND RAISE THE EMPLOYEE'S REAL EXPECTATION OF DETECTION.

There are three basic principles to achieve this requirement; denial, delay and deterrence.

Denial is the principle of a separation, that is the removal of the opportunity for unauthorised staff to have access to high theft risk assets. Access control systems and secure storage areas are the most obvious examples of this principle.

Delay is the principle of buying time, that is to allow direct access to high risk assets but to inhibit theft by making it difficult or obvious for, say, the article to be moved from its location, its carton or container to be readily opened, its price tickets to be removed, or for it to be easily concealed about the person or put into other containers.

Deterrence is the psychological principle of instilling into the mind of a potential thief a strong probability of detection, which may be strong enough to overcome the motivation to steal. Closed circuit television systems, electronic article surveillance systems, authorisation controls and bag and locker inspections all create an awareness that detection is a distinct possibility.

Employee theft prevention controls, having been developed and implemented must be audited regularly to ensure that they are in fact being maintained, and more importantly are effective. Like all policies and procedures, employee theft controls must be reviewed constantly to ensure they still meet the needs of the organisation's technological and operational requirements.

8. MAINTAIN A HIGHLY VISIBLE AND EFFECTIVE SYSTEM OF IDENTIFYING AND DETECTING OFFENDING EMPLOYEES AT ALL LEVELS OF THE ORGANISATION.

No matter how good the preventive measures taken, there are always those employees who will steal at any given opportunity regardless of the consequences. These employees must be detected, in order to both remove them from the workplace and to reinforce the probability of detection in the minds of other potential employee thieves. Detection is the fourth principle of theft prevention, and is utilised when the principles of deny, delay or deter have failed.

The detection of dishonest employees requires the use of highly trained and skilled investigators or loss prevention officers, often utilising specialised covert surveillance methods and equipment.

Law enforcement is the least cost effective method of theft prevention to implement and maintain, but is still widely practised by many major retailers in Australia. Law enforcement is a reactive function, loss prevention on the other hand is pro-active and committed to the prevention rather than the detection of theft and other forms of loss.

9. ENSURE THAT EMPLOYEE RELATIONS AND JOB SATISFACTION LEVELS ARE CONSTANTLY REVIEWED, AND IDENTIFIED PROBLEMS OR DEFICIENCIES CORRECTED.

There can be no doubt that job satisfaction and general employee relations are critical factors affecting the level of staff deviance. Dissatisfaction is not necessarily the product of poor pay and conditions or other material needs. It would seem to be more the employee's self esteem and sense of involvement, achievement, recognition and responsibility in and for the work they do, that affects their feelings towards their employer. Job satisfaction and stable employee relations are the product of good management and leadership. Poor examples and attitudes by management have a direct, detrimental effect on levels of theft in the workplace.

10. PROVIDE EMPLOYEES WITH THE OPPORTUNITY TO CONTRIBUTE TO THE LOSS PREVENTION INITIATIVES WITHIN THEIR PROFIT CENTRE; PROVIDE THE MEANS FOR COMMUNICATION ON ALL LOSS PREVENTION MATTERS.

There are a number of initiatives that can be taken to both involve staff directly in the loss prevention decision making process and to provide a means of communication on loss prevention matters, including the reporting of dishonest staff. Co-workers can be an effective deterrent to dishonest employees if they are prepared to participate in theft prevention efforts.

Honest staff, however, often find it difficult to accept that internal theft is actually occurring in their workplace, or if they are aware of theft going on about them, are reluctant to report it to management. Staff participation meetings are an effective way of helping employees form a strong opinion about internal theft and to make up their minds what to do about it. These meetings are conducted with groups of staff, where the problems of staff dishonesty are openly and honestly discussed, and employee attitudes and opinions are elicited and strengthened. Follow up meetings are held, and positive action plans developed.

Generally, two other initiatives follow on from the Participation Meetings. Store Loss Prevention Committees are formed, and communication links are established so that staff can report loss prevention matters openly or anonymously. Staff Participation Meetings are designed to strengthen employee awareness and commitment to reduce internal theft. Store Loss Prevention Committees are designed to foster management, staff and Loss Prevention co-operation to identify and reduce losses from all sources.

The in-store Loss Prevention Committee involves representatives from all areas of operation, including Loss Prevention. They meet on a regular basis and identify actual or potential loss factors, then develop cost effective controls to prevent or reduce those losses. A member of line management chairs these committee meetings so that action plans can be executed without reference to another level of authority.

Both the Staff Participation Meetings and the Loss Prevention committees are used to strengthen the internal theft prevention message, and useful information is communicated at these meetings Many staff, however, prefer to pass on information anonymously, and confidential facilities must be provided for this, either by way of a specified Post Office box number or telephone number.

Whether this service should be provided by external agencies or operated in-house is a matter that needs careful consideration, there are advantages and disadvantages in both methods, as there are having a continuously manned telephone, or an answering/recording device fitted.

Experience indicates that many calls received do not relate directly to dishonesty or other deviant acts, there are numerous complaints about management, working conditions, personnel problems etc. These should not be ignored, but treated as matters of concern, as they all point to areas of dissatisfaction in the workplace and should be eliminated.

CONCLUSION

Employees can be either profit makers or profit takers. The choice is clearly a matter of management perception of the nature and extent of the problem, and the ability to implement cost effective controls to prevent internal theft.

Aware, involved and motivated staff will not only be less inclined to steal from their employers, they will also act in a positive manner to protect their employer's assets from loss through internal and external causes. The foregoing ten initiatives, if used in a structured ongoing program, are the key to effective internal theft control.

SEMINAR: PREVENTING PROPERTY CRIME

List of Participants

Mr John Allsopp	Director Properties Department of Education PO Box 868 PARRAMATTA NSW 2150
Mr Victor A Anderson	Corporate Security Manager The Pratt Group 459 Collins Street MELBOURNE VIC 3000
Det Inspector Anstey	C.I.B. Tasmania Police 16 Magnet Court SANDY BAY TAS 7005
Mr Peter Beaver	Security Officer Dept of Transport and Communications GPO Box 367 CANBERRA CITY ACT 2601
Mr Ross Blowers	New Zealand Insurance 280 George Street SYDNEY NSW 2000
Mr Ray Brown	Managing Director Business Abuse Prevention System Pty Ltd Corporate House 50 Jolimont Street JOLIMONT VIC 3002
Ms Robyn Burgess	Criminal Law Review Division Attorney-General's Department GPO Box 6 SYDNEY NSW 2001
Mr Robert Butt	Neighbourhood Watch Area 39 29 Carbeen Street RIVETT ACT 2611
Mr Dennis Challinger	Assistant Director Australian Institute of Criminology PO Box 28 WODEN ACT 2606
Professor Duncan Chappell	Director Australian Institute of Criminology PO Box 28 WODEN ACT 2606

Mr Noel W Collins
Group Manager - Security
Pacific Dunlop
97 Flemington Road
NORTH MELBOURNE   VIC   3051

Mr Bob Coombs
8 Keele Street
WEST COMO   NSW   2226

Sergeant Chris Coster
Special Projects Officer
Victoria Police
380 William Street
MELBOURNE   VIC   3000

Mr Tom Devine
Neighbourhood Watch
33 Newdegate Street
DEAKIN   ACT   2600

Mr James Dolan
Group Leader
Neighbourhood Watch
11 Atherton Street
DOWNER   ACT   2602

Mr Victor Dorian
Manager, Corporate Security
 and Special Projects
Australian National Line
432 St Kilda Road
MELBOURNE   VIC   3001

Mr Kevin Dows
Risk Manager
McEwan's Pty Ltd
387-403 Bourke Street
MELBOURNE   VIC   3000

Mr Lionel Drake
Sales Manager
Chubb (Australia) Ltd
72 River Street
SOUTH YARRA   VIC   3141

Mr Danny Driscoll
Senior Sergeant
Australian Protective Services
Treasury Building
PARKES   ACT   2600

Mr Henry Edwards
QBE Insurance Ltd
PO Box 1008
CIVIC SQUARE   ACT   2608

Dr Paul Ekblom
Home Office Crime Prevention Unit
50 Queen Anne's Gate
LONDON   SW1H 9AT
UNITED KINGDOM

Mr Jim Fern	Director James S Fern and Associates 2/42 Premier Street NEUTRAL BAY NSW 2089
Mr Mark Flint	Legal Officer Director of Public Prosecutions PO Box E370 QUEEN VICTORIA TERRACE ACT 2600
Ms Julie Gardner	Project Officer Office of Crime Statistics GPO Box 464 ADELAIDE SA 5001
Mr John Garth	Security Manager CIG Gases 100 Christie Street ST LEONARDS NSW 2095
Ag/Commander B Hanney	W A Police Department 2 Adelaide Terrace EAST PERTH WA 6000
Mr Barry Harrison	Security Manager State Rail Authority Transport Investigation Branch 99 Macquarie Street SYDNEY NSW 2000
Mr James Hevey	Risk Control Surveyor GRE Insurance Ltd 6004 St Kilda Road MELBOURNE VIC 3004
Mr Andrew Hiller	Law Department University of Queensland ST LUCIA QLD 4067
Mr James Honan	Marketing Manager ADPRO Pty Ltd Innovation House West Technology Park THE LEVELS SA 5095
Sergeant 1/c J Hopgood	Crime Prevention Bureau Queensland Police Headquarters Makerston Street BRISBANE QLD 4000

Mr Chris Hudson	Manager Hudson's GPO Box 377 CANBERRA ACT 2601
Mr Graeme Ireland	Operations Manager MSS Guard Services 6 Kembla Street FYSHWICK ACT 2609
Mr David Ison	State Security Manager Woolworths Supermarkets 125 Main Street BLACKTOWN NSW 2148
Mr W F Jamieson	Chief Security Officer Telecom Australia 199 William Street MELBOURNE VIC 3000
Mrs Roberta Johnson	Secretary Neighbourhood Watch 7 Brand Street HUGHES ACT 2605
Sergeant Irene Juergens	O.I.C. New South Wales Police Crime Prevention Unit GPO Box 45 SYDNEY NSW 2000
Mr David Kerslake	Controller, Loss Prevention Coles Myer Ltd 762-838 Toorak Road TOORONGA VIC 3146
Mr George Kiddle	Coordinator Neighbourhood Watch 11 Gavin Place CHAPMAN ACT 2611
Mr Neville Kiely	National Marketing Manager Wormald Security Cnr Alexander and Ernest Streets CROWS NEST NSW 2065
Sergeant 1/c J King	Community Affairs Coordinator, Crime Western Australia Police Department 2 Adelaide Terrace EAST PERTH WA 6000

Mrs Rosslyn King

Personal Assistant to
President of Legislative Council
Parliament House
PERTH   WA   6000

Mr John Leeton

Neighbourhood Watch
MACKELLAR   ACT

Mr Brian Lillyman

Security Officer
Electricity Commission of NSW
PO Box 5257
SYDNEY   NSW   2001

Mr Roger Maskell

QBE Insurance Ltd
PO Box 1008
CIVIC SQUARE   ACT   2608

Ms Sylvia MacKellar

Australian Institute of Criminology
PO Box 28
WODEN   ACT   2606

Mr Brian McIlvenna

Chief Security Officer
Cockatoo Island Dockyard
C/- Post Office
ROZELLE   NSW   2039

Mr Laurie Monaghan

NRMA Insurance
151 Clarence Street
SYDNEY   NSW   2000

Mr Col Monger

Manager
MSS Guard Services
6 Kembla Street
FYSHWICK   ACT   2609

Mr Howard Murray

Executive Chief Superintendent
State Rail Authority
Transport Investigation Branch
99 Macquarie Street
SYDNEY   NSW   2000

Dr Satyanshu Mukherjee

Principal Criminologist
Australian Institute of Criminology
PO Box 28
WODEN   ACT   2606

Mr Robert Nelson

Marketing Manager for NSW
ADPRO Pty Ltd
Technology Park
THE LEVELS   SA   5095

Mr George Pitt

Sydney County Council
GPO Box 4009
SYDNEY   NSW   2001

Mr Alan Porter

Insurance Council of Australia
20 Bridge Street
SYDNEY   NSW   2000

Superintendent R J Potts

South Australia Police Department
Box 1539 GPO
ADELAIDE   SA   5001

Mr Russ Powell

Total Fire & Security (Aust) Pty Ltd
2 Leeds Street
CANTERBURY   VIC   3125

Ms Andrea Price

Systems Design Engineer
Adpro Pty Ltd
Innovation House West
Technology Park
THE LEVELS   SA   5095

Mrs Helena Prosser

Neighbourhood Watch
37 Millen Street
HUGHES   ACT   2605

Det. Sergeant Ransom

Anti Theft Branch
New South Wales Police Headquarters
14 College Street
SYDNEY   NSW   2000

Mr John Rice

National Loss Prevention Manager
Target (Australia) Pty Ltd
PO Box 41
NORTH GEELONG   VIC   3125

Mrs Elizabeth Richardson

Neighbourhood Watch Area 47
46 Beagle Street
RED HILL   ACT   2603

Mrs Glenys Rousell

Australian Institute of Criminology
PO Box 28
WODEN   ACT   2606

Mrs Judith Robertson

Neighbourhood Watch
6 Walker Crescent
GRIFFITH   ACT   2603

Mr Fergus Ross

Ranger Uranium Mines
PO Box 53
JABIRU   NT   5796

Mr Scott Ryrie

NRMA Insurance
151 Clarence Street
SYDNEY   NSW   2000

Mr Jack Sandry

OIC Publications
Australian Institute of Criminology
PO Box 28
WODEN   ACT   2606

Mr Rick Sarre

Lecturer
S.A. College of Advanced Education
Lorne Avenue
MAGILL   SA   5072

Mr Donald Shepherd

Neighbourhood Watch
9 Wise Street
BRADDON   ACT   2601

Mr Peter Smith

Neighbourhood Watch
53 Finniss Crescent
NARRABUNDAH   ACT   2604

Mrs Joy Steward

Accountant
PO Box 95
SOUTH YARRA   VIC   3141

Mr Bruce Swanton

Senior Research Officer
Australian Institute of Criminology
PO Box 28
WODEN   ACT   2606

Ms Julia Vernon

Programs Officer
Australian Institute of Criminology
PO Box 28
WODEN   ACT   2606

Mr Peter Ward

Principal Private Secretary
Office of the Minister for Police
170 St George's Terrace
PERTH   WA   6000

Mr Hugh Webb

Regional Loss Prevention Manager
Grace Bros Pty Ltd
33 Carter Street
LIDCOMBE   NSW   2141

Mr John Westbury

Insurance Council of Australia
31 Queen Street
MELBOURNE   VIC   3000

Mr Michael Wills   Assistant Director (Development)
                                    Properties Directorate
                                    Department of Education
                                    130 George Street
                                    PARRAMATTA NSW 2150

Mr Barry Wilson   Manager
                                    Connell, Campbell and Drew
                                    60 Albert Road
                                    SOUTH MELBOURNE VIC 3205

Dr Paul Wilson   Assistant Director (Research and Statistics)
                                    Australian Institute of Criminology
                                    PO Box 28
                                    WODEN ACT 2606

Mr Alan Woods   Coordinator Special Projects
                                    NSW Police Headquarters
                                    14-24 College Street
                                    SYDNEY NSW 2000